Jefferson Highway
All the Way

DENNY GIBSON

ISBN: 978-1796535280

ACKNOWLEDGMENTS

Thanks first to the folks who helped me plan this trip. That group included Lynda & Jerry Alger, Jane Ballard, Don Berger, Scott Burka, Mike & Sharon Curtis, Paul Gilger, Lyell D. Henry Jr., Highway Walkers Media (Darrell Johnston & Josiah Laubenstein), Russell S. Rein, and Glenn Smith. Scott, Mike, and Glenn also helped me during the trip as did Roger Bell. Mike Curtis helped even after the driving was done by reviewing the manuscript and heading off a variety of errors. I really appreciate everything everyone of you did.

Me, I want to live with my feet in Dixie
And my head in the cool blue North.

Jesse Winchester, *Nothing but a Breeze*, 1977

Contents

All Year Route

PRACTICALLY ALL

Hard Surfaced

FROM

Pine to Palm

Winnipeg to New Orleans

JEFFERSON HIGHWAY ALL THE WAY

THE JEFFERSON HIGHWAY traverses a country alluring in its opportunities for all season tours.

The recreation seekers' paradise—the wonderful lake region of Minnesota, with its densely shaded cool pine woods, has a strong appeal to folks who love the primitive.

The Jefferson Highway was originated in 1915 in New Orleans and is Louisiana's Own Highway; 85% of the roadway in this state is hard-surfaced; foremost Louisiana men assist in guiding the activities of the Association.

Our traveler's information bureau will aid you in planning your trip. Write today for maps and other literature regarding cities or points of interest reached by the International Jefferson Highway.

JEFFERSON HIGHWAY ASSOCIATION

HEADQUARTERS—TOOTLE BLDG.   ST. JOSEPH, MO.

MAPS FREE

LOMBY PRINTING CO., ST. JOSEPH, MO.

Cover of 1929 guide

1.   Birth

A little more than two years after the Lincoln Highway Association was formed to further Carl Fisher's ideas regarding a highway connecting the east and west coasts of the United States, a fellow named Edwin T. Meredith began talking up a highway honoring another president and running at right angles to the Lincoln. The LHA came into being in July of 1913. In the summer of 1915, Meredith was pushing for a highway spanning the nation north to south. In November of that year, the Jefferson Highway Association was formed to make such a road a reality. The name was chosen to honor President Thomas Jefferson who had been responsible for the Louisiana Purchase through which the proposed highway would run. Meredith was elected the organization's first president.

Meredith had selected endpoints for his proposed highway but not the path between them. The southern end of the route would be in New Orleans, Louisiana, where that November organizational meeting was held. The northern end would be in Winnipeg, Manitoba, Canada, making the Jefferson Highway one of just a handful of international named auto trails.

It will surprise no one that agreement on a path between points more than 1400 crow-miles apart did not come quickly or smoothly. Every city within a couple hundred miles of a line connecting the two anchor cities wanted to be on the highway. It took two days but that first meeting ended with an agreement on a list of "cardinal points" with the detailed paths between them to be decided by the organization's board of directors. From north to south, the "cardinal point" cities were Minneapolis, Saint Paul, Des Moines, Saint Joseph, Kansas City, Joplin, Muskogee, Denison, Shreveport, Alexandria, and Baton Rouge.

The words 'quick' and 'smooth' would not describe the February 1916 meeting of the directors in Kansas City, either. A few hundred uninvited guests more or less crashed the party to continue arguing for their favorite routes. The result was a plan that included a couple of alternate routes disguised as delayed decisions. Ending arguments by accepting both sides' positions is an age old technique that sure was common with the auto trails and it certainly didn't stop there. Consider all the numbered highways existing today with an 'N', 'S', 'E', or 'W' tacked on the end.

Places called Kansas City exist on both sides of the Kansas-Missouri line. The JHA clearly had the larger of the two in mind when they selected cardinal points, and boosters in both states seem to have accepted that Kansas, City, Missouri, was on the route. But they each had their own idea of how to get from there to Joplin. The Kansas folks wanted a route on their side of the line that went through Fort Scott and Pittsburg. The Missouri folk championed a route through Harrisonville and Carthage. The JHA directors recognized both.

Similarly, there were two views of how to plot the route north of Kansas City, although everybody seemed content to stay within Missouri. One group thought the JH should go through Saint Joseph and another favored Cameron. The JHA directors recognized both of these, too. The plan for both of these double routes was to eventually pick one or the other based on who improved their route the quickest. It does not, however, appear as if either of those decisions was ever made.

Eleven states were represented at the 1915 meeting in New Orleans. The initial route passed through just seven: Minnesota, Iowa, Missouri, Kansas, Oklahoma, Texas, and Louisiana. North Dakota, South Dakota, and Nebraska had been left off the route in favor of Minnesota and Iowa. That decision was essentially political and was no doubt influenced by the fact that Meredith's home was in Des Moines. Arkansas was left out because the existing roads through Oklahoma and Texas were significantly better.

Routing details certainly continued to change over the next several years but the basic shape of the highway established in 1916 remained constant through 1923.

1. Birth

1923 map from campground manual

At their February 1916 meeting, the directors identified a few "branch" routes. For the most part these seem to be extensions or feeders. An exception was a route Arkansas had proposed that ran from Joplin to Shreveport through the towns of Fort Smith and Texarkana. This is the route that had lost out to the one through Texas despite being much shorter. This was certainly not an extension or feeder but it was one of the branches identified at the very beginning.

By 1924 the condition of the roads in Arkansas had improved immensely, and the JHA officially recognized Arkansas as a member of the family. The state was allowed to define its own route and it chose an eastern course through Eureka Springs rather than the expected Texarkana route. Apparently the JHA didn't particularly care for Arkansas' choice, and when it created what was probably its final map in 1929, it was the border hugging route through Texarkana that was shown as one of two routes between Joplin and Shreveport. What was even more interesting, or at least more bizarre, was that the other official JH route between those two original "cardinal points" was not the familiar path through Bonham and Greenville, but a route that headed straight to Dallas from Denison. In Dallas, the new route turned due east to reach Shreveport.

Of course, all of those last minute changes were pretty much academic. The United States Numbered Highway System had come into being in 1926, and named auto trails such as the Jefferson Highway were a thing of the past. The JHA apparently still existed in 1929 and there must have been people who utilized its guide, but its importance was fading fast.

1. Birth

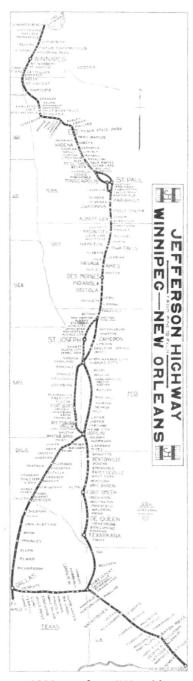

1929 map from JHA guide

2. Rebirth

The founding of the Lincoln Highway Association in 1913 had been part of Edwin T. Meredith's inspiration for forming the Jefferson Highway Association in 1915. Many decades later history would repeat itself but at a slower pace. A new LHA was formed in 1992 to promote and preserve the historic highway. The modern JHA was formed in 2011.

I was completely unaware of the Lincoln Highway Association when it reformed and barely aware of the highway. It was a strong and active organization by the time I joined in 2000. I was aware of the formation of the new Jefferson Highway Association, but did not join immediately. I finally joined in 2014, and by that time, it, too, was a strong and active organization.

I'm fairly certain I would have first learned of the Jefferson Highway around the turn of the century when I started developing an interest in historic highways and came across lists of named auto trails and other old roads. I did not look at it at all closely though because roads like the Lincoln and Dixie Highways were closer and much more likely to be driving targets for me. That changed in 2009 when I had my first real-life encounter with the Jefferson Highway.

While driving the western portion of the Lincoln Highway for the first time, I stopped at Reed-Niland Corner in Colo, Iowa. It happened to be a day when the cafe there was not open, but I could peer into the restored gas station and look over various signs on the property. Spotting some Jefferson

Highway Signs led me to the realization that two major cross-country auto trails had once met here.

By coincidence, 2009 was also the year when events that would lead to a new Jefferson Highway Association occurred. A Canadian named Mike Conlin had moved from Winnipeg to New Orleans where he became aware of the JH terminus marker at Common and Saint Charles and the highway that once connected his current and former homes. A desire to retrace the whole thing naturally developed and near the end of 2009 he headed to Winnipeg in order to meet a friend and follow the Jefferson Highway all the way back to New Orleans. As he researched the route, Conlin had found others who shared his interest, and in March 2011 many of them came together in Lee Summit, Missouri, to organize the new JHA with Conlin as its first president.

Regrettably, despite my awareness of this historic highway awakening at about the same time that a new association dedicated to it was coming to life, other activities kept me from paying it much attention. As should be expected with the birth of a new organization, the early years of the new Jefferson Highway Association saw some ups and downs. Things eventually leveled out, however, and when I attended my first JHA conference in 2015 in Muskogee, Oklahoma, what I saw was a smooth running organization thanks in large part to its then president, Glenn Smith, and his immediate predecessor, Theresa Russell.

I enjoy digging through old maps and guide books to a certain degree, but not nearly as much as I enjoy traveling the old roads they describe. One place where the dips and bumps of those first few years had a negative impact on the new organization was in documenting the path of the old road. A map or list of points of interest that covered the entire route simply did not exist, but there sure were pockets of activity and signs of progress.

One of the successes of the new Jefferson Highway Association was the publication of a quarterly newsletter, the *Jefferson Highway Declaration*, almost from day one. The name was taken from a monthly publication of the original JHA. In one of the first *Declaration*s I received after joining, mention of a recent full length drive caught my eye. JHA members Lynda and Jerry Alger had driven from Winnipeg to New Orleans in September 2014. The next issue carried Lynda's report of the trip. In it she identified many of the things to be seen along the way and described portions of their route. In plotting that route, the Algers employed a method with which I was very familiar: Identify places known to have been on the route then seek out old roads that connect them. It's a little bit like picking out ways to connect those "cardinal points" back in 1916.

Prior to the 2015 conference in Muskogee, Jane Ballard produced a Jefferson Highway tour guide for the entire state. Thanks to that guide, when I attended the conference I was able to do a miniature version of the trip covered by this book. I entered Oklahoma at its northern border, stopped for the conference somewhat short of the halfway mark, then drove to the Texas border after the conference. At the conference, there was buzz about ongoing mapping activities, an in progress book, and a possible documentary.

I also attended the 2016 JHA Conference in Carthage, Missouri. Driving directions for the JH in Jasper County were provided so I got to add several more miles to my score. There was a session on mapping at the conference although progress had been spotty. The documentary discussed in Muskogee was moving forward. The rumored book was complete.

The documentary would be produced by a pair of young filmmakers with a company called Highway Walkers Media. They would set out on a full length drive of the JH on May 8, just five days after the conference.

Lyell Henry's book, *The Jefferson Highway: Blazing the Way from Winnipeg to New Orleans,* was published just in time to be available at the conference. The book contains an excellent history of the original Jefferson Highway Association and the creation of the road plus details of the highway's path through Iowa.

I read Lyell's book as soon as I got home and watched the Highway Walker's documentary, *Less Traveled:A Journey from Pine to Palm*, soon after it was completed in September. Both cranked up my desire to drive the road myself by several notches, and the book provided the information needed to plot an accurate route through another state.

In 2017, other activities kept me from driving the Jefferson Highway or even attending the annual conference. There was a three part silver lining in that delay.

One part came from the Lincoln Highway Association. The LHA organized a tour for 2017 that began on the Lincoln Highway, but spent most of its time on the Jefferson Highway traveling from Colo, Iowa, to the northern terminus in Winnipeg. In support of the tour, LHA map committee chairman Paul Gilger produced a map of their route. That added directions for Minnesota and Manitoba to those available to me.

The second piece of the silver lining was the location of the 2018 JHA Conference. Road trips obviously don't need to be tied to conferences or any other sort of gathering, but it can be kind of fun if they are. The 2018 conference location was Saint Joseph, Missouri. This is nearly the highway's midpoint which is one of the reasons JHA headquarters were moved there from Des Moines, Iowa, in 1918. Another reason for the move was that the Pikes Peak Ocean-to-Ocean Highway also passed through the city and operations for the two highways were combined in Saint Joseph that year. Celebrating the 100th anniversary of the move was a key part of the decision to have the 2018 JHA Conference there.

My planning for an end-to-end drive centered around the conference was already underway when the third bit of silver lining was revealed. JHA Vice President Mike Curtis, who would follow part of the JH to the Saint Joseph conference from the south, completed and shared his full length JH map shortly before my planned departure.

In a smashup of metaphors, that last bit of silver lining was the frosting on the cake. The Algers had undertaken their 2014 trip without having many details of the old road's path available. By contrast I was blessed with quite a bit of information that had appeared since then. There was Jane Ballard's set of directions through Oklahoma and the Iowa route details in Lyell Henry's 2016 book. The Highway Walkers' documentary gave me another view of what a full length drive entailed, and Paul Gilger's 2017 tour guide helped me nail down the route in Minnesota and Manitoba. Mike and Sharon Curtis had driven to the 2017 JHA Conference in Denison, Texas, from the highway's southern terminus, and had shared their route which allowed me to plot my course through Texas and Louisiana. The remaining gaps were filled and the cake frosted when Mike announced completion of his full length map.

I communicated with Lynda, Paul, Mike, and others right up to and beyond my departure. I'm guessing that I had about as accurate a version of the old Jefferson Highway route as anyone driving the whole thing since the 1920s or

'30s, but I know that the next person doing it will have an even more accurate and complete version. I wish that next person, and those that follow, lots of luck. They will have better directions when they begin, and there's a good chance they will track the old route more closely than I did, but I doubt they'll enjoy it any more. Let me tell you about it.

3.   Manitoba

Before I could actually start driving the Jefferson Highway I had to get to one end or the other. Wanting to drive the route in the traditional north-to-south Pine-to-Palms direction, I set out off for Winnipeg, Manitoba, smack dab in the middle of April. My not overly precise calculations indicated that this was the latest I should leave home in order to make the opening of the conference on the 26th. The 1100 mile drive was spread over three days. I chose the fastest route available which meant mostly expressways. At Mason City, Iowa, I deviated from the absolute fastest route to enter the town and experience a hotel that would not be available when I returned on the Jefferson Highway. With one exception, I will include my northbound Mason City experiences with my southbound Mason City experiences in the proper geographic but improper chronological sequence. In other words, I'll tell you about them in a couple of chapters.

There had actually been a little snow in the air as I was preparing to leave Cincinnati. It wasn't really sticking to the ground and it was moving rapidly to the east so I just waited for it to pass. I saw several leftover piles of the white stuff and even a few light flurries as I drove through Indiana and Illinois and into Iowa, but things were still looking good when I reached Mason City. They were not going to stay that way.

Snow storm, Mason City, IA (Apr 18, 2018)

When I bedded down for the night, snowfall of 1 to 2 inches per hour was predicted to hit about 4:00 AM. I briefly considered getting up in the middle of the night to escape the approaching storm, but was too tired and lazy to actually take any steps to accomplish that. On awakening, I jumped to the window to see no new snow on the ground and none in the air. I was quickly packed and ready to go but decided to have breakfast at the hotel. That was not the smartest thing I've ever done.

The snow predicted for 4:00 had merely been delayed a few hours. It was just starting to fall when I finally did pull out around 8:00. By the time I drove through town and turned west toward the expressway, the scene in the photo was in front of me and the rate of snowfall was increasing. It was initially even worse on I-35 but traffic kept some tracks open and I eventually found myself north of the storm. The radio said Mason City might see 5 to 8 inches before it was all over.

As I hinted earlier and as the Iowa storm reinforced, mid-April is just a wee bit early in the year for vacationing in Canada and the northern United States. The dates had essentially been dictated by my decision to organize the trip around the JHA conference in Saint Joseph. I could have lessened the impact of the season by driving the opposite direction and saving the most northern segments for May but I had reasons for doing it as I did and I don't regret it a bit. However, I do suggest hitting the northern end of the Jefferson Highway sometime beyond April if possible.

The Forks, Winnipeg, MB (Apr 19, 2018)

The storm I ran away from in Iowa was the only "live" snow that I saw on the trip, but I did see some good sized mounds of the stuff and the effects of some that had recently melted. I had an afternoon in Winnipeg and spent a portion of it in an area known as The Forks. It's something of a combination park, market, and entertainment district. Some parts of the park area were still fenced off for winter and some that were open were still buried under snow or muddy from the runoff.

Canadian Museum for Human Rights, Winnipeg, MB (Apr 19, 2018)

The market area, however, was going strong with plenty of open shops and food stands. I ate lunch there and did some people watching before walking past the Canadian Museum for Human Rights and back to the car.

In the morning, I finally began my trip on the highway named for our third president. Thomas Jefferson is recognized as a prominent historic figure in Canada but not to the same degree as in the country that he helped found. Using his name to reference the highway did not come as naturally there as in the USA. Canadians referred to it by what their neighbors used more as a nickname: The Pine to Palm Highway.

Bank of Montreal/Start of JH, Winnipeg, MB (Apr 20, 2018)

Pine to Palm Highway marker, Winnipeg, MB (Apr 20, 2018)

In addition to the name, at least one other distinction may exist between the two. Although nothing official has been found, there are reasons to believe that early travelers thought of the intersection of Main Street and Portage

Avenue in Winnipeg as the northern end of the Jefferson Highway. A sign stating "No. 1 Jefferson Highway" once stood there and other routes to Winnipeg ended there. There does not,however, appear to be a JH related marker of any sort at the intersection now. The southeast corner does hold an impressive Bank of Montreal building that was only a couple of years old when the JH was born.

Winnipeg mayors have twice led caravans from their city to New Orleans along the path of the Jefferson/Pine to Palm Highway. Mayor Ralph Webb, a retired military officer, did it in 1926. Mayor Stephen Juba did it in 1957. Both caravans started a few miles south of downtown Winnipeg on the Pembina Highway. To commemorate the 75th anniversary of the first caravan, a marker was erected near that starting point in 1974. The marker identifies the spot as "the northern end of the Pine to Palm Highway". I began my own drive at Main and Portage but made sure to stop at the Pembina Highway marker.

I was in a clean car as I did my drive by of the bank and paused at the marker. Snow and slush on the drive north had really done a job on the car's windows and visibility was severely hampered. I had a pretty good idea of the sort of roads I'd be seeing once I started south, and a sensible part of me knew I should just clear the windows as best I could at the next gas stop. But some other part just couldn't resist pulling into the open car wash I spotted on the way to the motel. I looked good and could see good as I worked my way through the morning traffic.

Clean car on first encounter with unpaved JH, Apr 20, 2018

My intention was to follow any and all of the original Jefferson Highway that I was aware of and which was passable. I knew that would include a full range of unpaved surfaces so I wasn't at all surprised or reluctant to proceed when I came to a gravel section about a dozen miles south of the Pine to Palm marker. I did, however, feel a need to record the moment so I could prove that I'd started out clean.

Note the new Jefferson Highway magnet on the door. I'd received the pair (There's one on the other side, too.) shortly before leaving home and had arranged for a backup set to be waiting for me in Saint Joseph. They were not needed as the set that went on in Winnipeg were still there when I reached New Orleans.

I believe this approximately eight mile long segment was the longest unpaved stretch I saw in Canada. Before crossing the border, I would accumulate 32 unpaved miles of 72 total. All of them were pretty much like the road in the picture, smooth, level, and well maintained. In fact, some of the dust I accumulated on this and another section was stirred up by graders actively maintaining the road.

Union Point Church, MB (Apr 20, 2018)

I passed through the town of Saint Agathe on asphalt then drove another mile or so of gravel before being forced back on Provincial Trunk Highway 75. The gravel sections exist because they were bypassed by PTH 75 many years ago. Other parts were covered including the town of Union Point. The town was pretty much gone by the time the road became divided 4-lane in the 1980s. About all that was left was the 1940 church, built to replace an 1887 structure that had burned the year before, and its cemetery. Had it been just the church, it probably would have been leveled and paved over. The cemetery saved it, and the southbound lanes of the expressway bow just enough to leave the church, and the graves beside it, intact between them and the ones leading north.

Road grader near Morris, MB (Apr 20, 2018)

After a dozen miles of modern paved expressway, I turned back onto gravel at the town of Morris. Here, for the second time of the day, I encountered a road grader hard at work. It had the road blocked, but I'd been looking forward to this section and had no intention of skipping it. The grader and I were moving the same direction so I simply alternated between pausing at the side of the road and inching along it. The reason I had been looking forward to driving this road was that it was a second generation alignment, with an older abandoned alignment to its east. Although the older alignment could not be driven, three of its bridges were visible from both the road I was driving and the several lanes of PTH 75 to the west. They would also have been visible to anyone on the Canadian National Railway tracks running between PTH 75 and the other roads.

Abandoned bridge near Morris, MB (Apr 20, 2018)

Abandoned bridge near Morris, MB (Apr 20, 2018)

I thought the middle of the three bridges the most interesting looking and that's the one shown in both pictures. The date 1924 can be seen clearly on the southernmost bridge and a not so clear date on the northernmost bridge is likely the same. There is virtually no doubt that these bridges were in use during the Jefferson Highway's heyday.

Former site of Saint Pie Church, MB (Apr 20, 2018)

The bridges I expected; The cross was a surprise. The towns of Saint Jean Baptiste and Letellier lie between the old bridges and the US border. The road is paved through the towns but not between them. The cross stands alone at some distance from the gravel road. It is rather striking in the middle of an empty field. My first thought was that it was all that was left of something, but the truth is that it was put there as a standalone marker for something that was already gone.

The Saint Pie Catholic Church was established here in 1880 and moved to Letellier in 1891. The cross was erected in 1924. I believe the original building burned although there is a Church of Saint Pie currently in Letellier. We're five years away from the centennial of a cross erected for a church that moved on thirty-three years earlier after standing here for eleven years. An unusual sight and story.

Fort Dufferin, MB (Apr 20, 2018)

My last stop in Canada was at Fort Dufferin. Between 1872 and 1879, Fort Dufferin played an important role in Canada's development. It was home base for the country's International Boundary Commission members, served as headquarters for the North West Mounted Police (today's Royal Canadian Mounted Police), and was the gateway for immigrants entering the country on the Red River.

There was really no activity here in the early spring. The few buildings there were closed, and the ground was too wet to do much exploring. I did benefit from one feature of the site, however. As I would be traveling from pine to palm, I had planned to photograph some majestic pine tree in Winnipeg to represent the northern end of the journey. I'd totally forgotten to do that but fortunately remembered while I was still in Canada. With appropriate solemnity, I paused at the entrance and silently designated the pictured pair of trees my official "from pines" for the trip.

4. Minnesota

In the old days, the Jefferson Highway crossed the international border through the towns of Emerson, Manitoba, and Noyes, Minnesota. That crossing has been closed since 2006 so that a detour off of the Jefferson Highway and through a corner of North Dakota is required.

Border crossing at Pembina, ND (Apr 20, 2018)

In hindsight, I kind of wish I'd driven the old road as close as possible to each side of the border but I didn't. I entered the US at the Pembina station then turned east at the first opportunity. I was in North Dakota for 3.3 miles. No chapter for you, ND.

Former Jefferson Highway, St Vincent, MN (Apr 20, 2018)

About half a mile after entering Minnesota, I was reunited with paved Jefferson Highway at the north edge of the town of Saint Vincent, and a half mile after that I was reunited with unpaved Jefferson Highway. Initially the unpaved surface was well maintained gravel like I had been driving for much of the day, but, somewhere near the south edge of town, the gravel seemed to vanish along with evidence of recent maintenance.

I couldn't help noticing that the change in the quality of unpaved roads had coincided with the crossing of the border although I knew that wasn't the reason. Proof that Minnesota doe not ignore its dirt and gravel roads appeared later that same day when I encountered a grader working on another bit of unpaved Jefferson Highway. Each country and each state and province has to deal with road maintenance based on available resources and local needs. Many of the roads I drive are roads without many users and are therefore not high on the priority list.

There is no real shortage of paved roads in the area, and it wasn't long until the Jefferson Highway and I hooked up with US 75 for a few miles. In the town of Hallock, I turned east onto MN 175.

Gateway Motel and Museum, Hallock, MN (Apr 20, 2018)

I had worked backwards from the conference date to determine a departure date, and that meant I had also determined where I would be on all the days in between. This schedule was essentially in place before I learned of the Gateway Motel in Hallock. It was about half a mile beyond the turnoff, and I knew I wouldn't be staying there, but that didn't stop me from taking a peek. Yep, that's definitely a place I'd like to stay someday.

From Hallock, I followed something of a stair-step path to Karlstad. Karlstad calls itself "The Moose Capital of the North", and advertises the claim with several statues and images around town. There's a smiling face – of a moose –

on the water tower. I once again slipped off the Jefferson Highway just a bit to see the big moose statue that greets visitors arriving on US 59.

Moose statue, Karlstad, MN (Apr 20, 2018)

Sign on Historical Pembina Trail Road, Karlstad, MN (Apr 20, 2018)

I left Karlstad on asphalt, but turned onto gravel about four miles outside of town. The road is signed as "Historical Pembina Trail Road", and despite the "MINIMUM MAINTENANCE" sign was in very good condition. In fact, this is where I met the working grader mentioned earlier.

Chateau Inn, Red Lake Falls, MN (Apr 21, 2018)

I covered approximately ten miles of gravel before hitting a forty mile stretch of asphalt that took me through Thief River Falls and within ten miles of the day's destination. That destination was an independent motel in Red Lake Falls. On the way, I picked up an older alignment and a few miles of gravel that took me to the town. My room at Chateau Inn was clean and comfortable and situated above a liquor store. All three were positives to me but you can do your own scoring.

Unpaved road near Bagley, MN (Apr 21, 2018)

Jefferson sign near Solway, MN, (Apr 21, 2018)

Although I would see a fair amount of unpaved road during my second day on the Jefferson Highway, the day started with thirty some miles of asphalt. The pictured road near Bagley was the third unpaved section I encountered and the first with even a hint of being treacherous. The first two were level and dry, and I attribute the slippery conditions here to melting snow and not to a lack of maintenance. These unpaved roads are not ignored. As can be seen, the snow here, and on other unpaved segments I drove, had been plowed to the side.

The slippery curve was a few miles north of Bagley. The Jefferson sign is on another unpaved segment about ten miles east. It is the first sign I spotted bearing the name Jefferson. The town of Solway is just a couple of miles beyond.

Typical Minnesota gravel road near Solway, MN (Apr 21, 2018)

To anyone flipping through this book and just looking at pictures, it probably seems like I'm really bashing Minnesota roads. I certainly don't mean to, and I feel an obligation to include an example of what the vast majority of the state's unpaved roads look like. This photo of a dry and nicely graded piece of one time Jefferson Highway was taken roughly two miles east of Solway.

The state of Minnesota contains two attractions I've wanted to see since I was a kid. Today I would see them both in quick succession, and the fact that I was doing it while following the Jefferson Highway was an extra bonus.

Paul Bunyan & Babe, Bemidji, MN (Apr 21, 2018)

The first of the two attractions to come off of my to-do list was the eighteen foot tall Paul Bunyan and his partner, Babe the Blue Ox in Bemidji. Since their creation in 1937, both Paul and Babe have been treated to several repaints and refurbishings, and Babe, after two years as a mostly canvas covered portable parade participant, was transformed to the very solid and quite immobile lakeside fixture we know today.

Niiemii, Bemidji, MN (Apr 21, 2018)

Although Bemidji was a place I had long been aware of, I didn't really know a thing about it beyond it being home to statues representing a pair of American folk legends. I enjoyed lunch and a local brewery there. In walking around town I discovered that it is a city that appreciates its local artists. Examples stand on many of its street corners. Niiemii ("He Dances"), is not on a corner but in the same lakeside park as the iconic statues of Paul and Babe.

I was approaching the next long listed to-do item barely an hour after leaving Bemidji. The Jefferson Highway had missed Paul and Babe by a few years and a couple of blocks. My second targeted attraction had once flowed directly under the historic highway. A rather short bridge had carried the original alignment of the JH over the headwaters of the Mississippi River.

I've seen plenty of pictures of people crossing the mighty Mississippi on a few rocks or just wading through the shallow water at the river's beginning. I've no doubt imagined I might

39

do the same someday but this would not be the day. The closest I came to wading was slogging through the melting snow on the walk to the Lake Itasca shore. This was just another consequence of traveling through the north in early spring, and didn't reduce the awe of seeing the river I've crossed on super long bridges where it's just a few feet wide and a few inches deep.

Path to Mississippi headwaters, Itasca SP, MN (Apr 21, 2018)

Mississippi headwaters, Istaca SP, MN (Apr 21, 2018)

The white stuff in the background of both preceding photos is ice on the surface of Lake Itasca. The three barely visible white dots are swans who seemed to be enjoying their cool float and finding plenty of chilled edibles just below the surface. The string of rocks marks the point where water leaves the lake to become part of a river and begin its own pine to palm journey. In warmer times, people often cross the Mississippi on these rocks or slip off of them into it. No one did either today although a couple of people did step onto the first rock and think about it. I didn't even think about it, but did cross the river a short distance downstream where a tree trunk was used to form a bridge.

People sometimes give me a hard time about the speed at which I travel. Those that do claim taking three days just to drive across Ohio is excessive. Authorities say that it takes an average of three months for water to travel from Lake Itasca to the Gulf of Mexico. I would make it in fifteen days. Seems fast enough to me.

Although my plotted course could not exactly match that of the original Jefferson Highway through Itasca State Park, I did intend to mimic its basic straight through the park approach. I had entered the park via the north entrance as planned, but, when I headed for the south entrance, I found the way blocked by snow near Douglas Lodge. I left the park through the east entrance and made my way to US 71.

St Urho, Menahga, MN (Apr 21, 2018)

I stayed with US 71 through Park Rapids then started stair-stepping on secondary roads at the south edge of town. I returned to US 71 north of Menahga where I paused to learn about the totally fictitious but nonetheless interesting Saint Urho. According to legend (which originated in the 1950s) Saint Urho drove the grasshoppers out of Finland, but there are indications that he might not have been completely successful.

I left US 71 to drive through the town of Sebeka and again a short time later to angle southwest toward my end of day stop in Wadena. The road got a little interesting along the way.

CR-127, Wadena County, MN (Apr 21, 2018)

I again need to stress that most of the unpaved roads in Minnesota look like that nicely graded dry stretch near Solway that appeared a few pages back. But I also need to include a picture of a pretty bad looking stretch north of Wadena. The reason I feel the need to share this photo is that it shows the warm-up to what I believe was the worst section of road encountered on the entire trip. I have no pictures of that actual section because I was too busy driving to take pictures, but I assure you that it was considerably worse than what I did get a picture of. Once again it was melting snow causing the ruts and mud.

Brookside Motel, Wadena, MN (Apr 21, 2018)

The town of Wadena was just a few miles beyond my little mud and rut run-in, and the motel where I'd booked a room was just about a mile back north on US 71. The Brookside Motel was another independent; This one operated by an actual mom and pop. No liquor store this time but the knotty-pine paneled room was clean and comfortable.

In the morning, I had a good breakfast in Wadena then headed on to Little Falls. I struck gravel within minutes but fears born of yesterday's encounter were unwarranted. All three sections I encountered were dry and rutless. As it turned out, all of the day's unpaved roadway was behind me by the time I reached Little Falls where I found that a 1930s era gas station I'd been looking forward to seeing was closed.

Crowder Station, Little Falls, MN (Apr 22, 2018)

The Crowder family has been operating the station that bears their name since 1935. People who have visited the station describe it as something of a time capsule. I anticipated an interesting visit and fun chat with current station master Brian Crowder but it was not to be. There was no explanation on the building, but I learned later that Brian had taken ill. The closure was expected to be short lived but the station continues to be reported closed at the time of writing.

A surprise in Saint Cloud made a huge dent in the disappointment of finding Crowder's Station closed. Getting caught by the light probably helped since I otherwise might have driven right on by without even noticing the tiny building on the corner. To be honest, it was probably the crowd of people that first caught my eye and not the building itself. Even after the forced study time, I attempted to drive on when the light changed but just could not do it. This place looked much too interesting, and I turned back in less than two blocks.

Val's Rapid Serv, St Cloud, MN (Apr 22, 2018)

What I found when I parked and stepped inside was not quite like anything I'd seen before. The place was packed and it wasn't with people dawdling over their meals. The sign says "Take Out Service" and it means it. There are no tables in the one time Pure Oil station. Some customers eat in their cars; Most carry their 'burger filled sacks home, back to work, or to some other interesting spot. Those sacks are handed out by a single employee at the only opening in a glass wall that allows a view of the cooking and bagging areas.

Orders reach the kitchen in one of two ways. Some are called in by telephone. When those orders are ready, the person at the window calls out the name and collects payment. Most orders, however, are placed through the five touchscreen kiosks placed against the walls. Most are paid for with credit cards or discounted prepaid Val's cards but cash is an option. Meals paid for with plastic are simply picked up when the identifying number is called. Cash payments are collected and change returned at the pickup window. The skill set required to work that window is remarkable and the smooth flow of the whole operation sure is impressive.

Val's Rapid Serv, St Cloud, MN (Apr 22, 2018)

The Rapid Serv name once identified a loosely formed regional franchise. Val's, which opened in 1959 and is still owned and operated by the same family, is the last of the breed. Apparently Val's once used telephones for placing orders, and that may have been part of the Rapid Serv brand, but I don't know that. I do know that 12:30 on a Sunday afternoon is a great time to catch an impressive show that blends 1950s fast food and 21st century technology. And I do know that the hamburgers, one of which I ate in my car, are darned good.

My drive through Champlin included a short bit of a street still named Jefferson Highway. I spent the night a little northwest of Minneapolis and drove into the city in the morning. Despite avoiding it on two previous visits and telling myself I would do the same this time, I caved and did a drive-by of the statue of Mary Tyler Moore tossing her hat in the air. One Twin Cities' icon I had no intention of missing was Mickey's Dining Car. I went straight from Mary to Mickey's for breakfast.

Mickey's Dining Car, St Paul, MN (Apr 23, 2018)

Reportedly, Mickey's Dining Car has been open – 24/7/365 – ever since Mickey Crimmons and Bert Mattson opened the Jerry O'Mahoney built diner in 1939. The food was great, the service friendly, and the whole experience just a whole lot of fun.

While I was there, I overheard two of the employees discussing a recently opened nearby martini bar. Apparently the new place served food and they wondered if it would hurt or help their business.

"We need a martini bar here," one suggested.

"We sure do," agreed the other. "For employees only."

My last stop before the state line was in Northfield where the James-Younger Gang effectively ceased to be. Their attempt to rob the First National Bank was met with resistance that left two gang members dead along with two of the locals. Although the dead included neither a James nor a Younger, and Jesse James would organize another gang after a few years, two of the Youngers were wounded and the gang dissolved.

Former First National Bank, Northfield, MN (Apr 23, 2018)

The bank building is now part of the Northfield Historical Society Museum. Among the exhibits on local history, including the attempted robbery, is a B.Y.O.B story of a different sort. One of the dead robbers, Clell Miller, was shot by a nineteen year old Henry Wheeler, apparently at home on a break from his medical studies at the University of Michigan. Back at school, and finding it difficult to obtain a cadaver as an aid to his education, Henry wrote home and someone dug up the robbers and shipped them to Ann Arbor in barrels marked "paint". When asked how he had obtained a cadaver, Henry answered simply and truthfully, "I shot him."

Northfield sits about sixty five miles from the state line. Almost all of those miles are paved and the few that aren't were dry and smooth when I passed over them. The run to the border was extremely pleasant in 65 degree sunshine, and the closest thing I had to excitement was having to hastily close all the windows when I unexpectedly hit some gravel and stirred up a cloud of dust.

Minnesota-Iowa line (Apr 23, 2018)

5. Iowa

Yes, the first picture in this chapter does look a lot like the last picture in the previous chapter. It should, of course. It's just the other side of the same marker.

Minnesota-Iowa line (Apr 23, 2018)

Although it is a slight anachronism, the plaque on the marker references the Jefferson Highway. Technically, the Jefferson Highway, and other named auto trails, ceased to exist when the United States Numbered Highway System was approved on November 11, 1926. The marker was dedicated nearly four years later yet it celebrates the completion of the

Jefferson Highway across the two states sharing the border. It was a goal established years before, and they weren't about to let officialdom's move from names to numbers keep them from recognizing it being reached.

Plaque at Minnesota-Iowa line (Apr 23, 2018)

The next few paragraphs and pictures may cause something of a time warp, too, but I can explain. Back in chapter 3, when I wrote about encountering snow in Mason City, I said I would tell about the rest of my northbound Mason City experiences at the same time as my southbound experiences. That time is now.

The background is that I wanted to stay in a particular hotel in Mason City but it was fully booked on all days I might have worked it into my southbound drive through the city on the Jefferson Highway. However, in the middle of my drive to the north end of the highway, I made a call and found that a room was available for the night I would be passing close by. I booked the room and checked out some other Mason City points of interest while I was there. I'll pick up the southbound trip immediately following a few items from the earlier visit.

Suzie-Q Cafe, Mason City, IA (Apr 17, 2018)

I arrived in Mason City too early to check into the hotel but the time did not go to waste. For starters, I headed to the Suzie-Q Cafe for one of their famous pork tenderloins. When Troy, the owner, asked if I needed a menu, I replied, "Probably not". "Guess that means a tenderloin," he said. Troy is a funny and friendly guy who also cooks a mean tenderloin. His workplace is a ten seat 1948 Valentine Little Chef.

Meredith Willson was born in Mason City, and the composer's childhood home is part of Music Man Square. I used the rest of my extra time walking around the area and snapping a few photos but I did not tour the home.

Meredith Willson birthplace, Mason City, IA (Apr 17, 2018)

Historic Park Inn, Mason City, IA (Apr 17, 2018)

The hotel I was so anxious to stay at is the Historic Park Inn, the only Frank Lloyd Wright designed hotel in existence. Combining a hotel, bank, and office space, the building opened in 1910, but the original glory days did not last long.

The bank failed in 1921, and that portion of the building was altered quite a bit in 1926. The hotel declined and was eventually turned into apartments. The slide continued until the building sat empty.

Historic Park Inn, Mason City, IA (Apr 17, 2018)

In 2005, a non-profit organization called Wright at the Park was formed to save the landmark, and a major renovation project culminated in the hotel reopening in 2011. The renovation brought in all the modern amenities expected in a top rank hotel without destroying any of the Frank Lloyd Wright elegance or the building's historic feeling. Dinner at the onsite 1910 Grille was excellent, and that's also where I had the breakfast that allowed the snow to almost catch me in the morning. The Historic Park Inn wasn't the cheapest lodging of my trip but it was one of the most enjoyable. I'm definitely happy that I got to work it in.

I will now return to the southbound drive and discussing things in the proper order. The flashback is over.

Birdsall's Ice Cream, Mason City, IA (Apr 23, 2018)

Although they are close, neither the Historic Park Inn nor the Suzie-Q Cafe are right on the Jefferson Highway. Birdsall's Ice Cream is. Birdsall's was on my to-do list, and I'd thought about it during my earlier visit, but there just wasn't room – time or tummy wise – to fit it in. Instead, it became the first place I stopped when I returned to Mason City on the JH. This northern Iowa icon has been making ice cream since 1931, and I can attest to the chocolate being top grade. I had mine with marshmallow and chopped pecans.

There was one more not-quite-on-the-JH attraction in the city that I intended to visit but it would wait. My next stop would be several miles from Mason City and well off of the Jefferson Highway. Despite its lack of connection with the trip's primary purpose, it was a place I had no intention of missing now that I was this close.

Surf Ballroom, Clear Lake, IA (Apr 23, 2018)

The Surf Ballroom in Clear Lake is associated more with music fans than with road fans. It's where Buddy Holly played his last show on February 2, 1959.

Surf Ballroom, Clear Lake, IA (Apr 23, 2018)

Inside, there are displays and plenty of reminders of that day. The venue, however, continues to operate and remains both successful and relevant. I've little doubt that the stage, dance floor, and booths appear very much the same as they did when The Crickets and The Belmonts played here.

Although I'd never actually been there before, it all felt a little familiar. I've seen pictures, of course, and that was certainly part of the reason. But I think maybe a bigger part was the fact that I'd seen and spent some of my youth in similar looking venues, and simply experienced a brief flashback of my own.

Not only do I remember venues like the Surf Ballroom, I remember learning about the plane crash that killed Holly, J.P. Richardson, Ritchie Valens, and Roger Peterson. I was beside my sister in the back seat of the family's 1954 Dodge when the AM radio brought the news. As a twelve year old, I was more upset by the loss of Richardson than Holly. Richardson was The Big Bopper, and just having a nickname like that was cool. His songs were also cool and funny, and pulling out your deepest pre-teen voice to sing along with "You know what I like" from *Chantilly Lace* could make you feel cool, too.

Holly crash site marker near Clear Lake, IA (Apr 23, 2018)

I drove a few miles north of Clear Lake to the big black glasses that mark a path to the actual crash site. As I pondered whether or not to make the walk, two men came walking back along the fence. Only one had actually made it to the site. The other had stopped halfway because of mud. I decided to not even start.

Rancho Deluxe Z Garden, Mason City, IA (Apr 24, 2018)

After spending the night in Clear Lake, I headed back to Mason City to check out that one more attraction I mentioned. I have no idea what the 'Z' means or even if it's really part of the name. The closest thing to an official online presence the garden has, a Facebook page, doesn't include it but almost every other online reference to the place does. The Facebook page is "Rancho Deluxe – The Original Bicycle Garden". Max Weaver, a former Mason City council member, built the garden predominately from discards. One article quotes him as saying, "As Mason City tore itself down during the 70s and 80s, I was there to pick it up." Artists like Weaver tend to make uptight people uncomfortable, and politically astute and active ones, which Weaver appears to be, doubly so. I didn't meet Mr. Weaver when I visited his garden but I'd like to. He sounds like a very interesting guy and maybe I could ask him about the 'Z'.

Rock of Ages, Rockwell, IA (Apr 24, 2018)

Another bit of folk art appeared about ten miles south of Mason City. Rock of Ages is in the town of Rockwell and actually on the Jefferson Highway.

JH barn near Hubbard, IA (Apr 24, 2018)

There is a barn south of Hubbard with more of a Jefferson Highway connection than just standing beside it. Painted high on the barn's side is the year "1917" and the name "Jefferson Highway Farm". The barn could clearly use a little paint and attention but it faces much more imminent danger than slow deterioration. The farm's current owner has plans to raze the barn but he is willing to cooperate in it being moved. At the time of writing, the Hubbard Historical Society was close to finalizing arrangements to relocate the barn to a spot within Hubbard.

JH post near Colo, IA (Apr 24, 2018)

That barn is hard to miss. This post is hard to find – for some of us. I drove the road and walked the road. I returned to my car, reread every clue I had, and walked the road again. At last I found the conjoined J and H of the Jefferson Highway in an actual fence post with an eye bolt dead center. It is on the southwest corner of US 65 and 210th Street about two miles north of Colo. I'd been ignoring that particular post because I was not expecting the marker to be part of a

fence. It's a combination of esteem and pragmatic irreverence not often seen, and, for reasons not at all clear to me, I like it.

Reed-Niland Corner, Colo, IA (Apr 24, 2018)

I know I raved about the Historic Park Inn in Mason City but Reed-Niland Corner near Colo was actually my favorite overnight stop of the whole trip. When they first met here, the Jefferson and Lincoln Highways traveled together to the town of Nevada seven miles to the west. There the Jefferson turned south. A route change in 1921 extended their time together by moving the Jefferson's turn eight miles beyond Nevada to the town of Ames. There is no question that this spot, where two nation wide auto trails met, once had a very legitimate claim to being the Crossroads of America.

I reached the corner for the first time by traveling west on the Lincoln Highway. I had seen the Jefferson Highway on old maps and lists of named auto trails, but encountering the road here in 2009 was the first time I had ever thought of the road as something real that I might interact with.

Charlie Reed started things off by opening a gas station in 1923. Before long, his nephew, Clare Niland, opened a cafe and some tourists cabins. The cabins were replaced in the 1940s by the row of motel rooms there now.

The gas station looks like it could sell gas today but it doesn't. Restored to its 1920s appearance, it's something of a museum. The motel and cafe are very active businesses. The cafe is also a museum with informative displays on the Lincoln and Jefferson and their modern counterparts, US 30 and US 65. The corner is still something of a one-stop except now it supplies history, food, and lodging instead of gas, food, and lodging.

Looking north from Reed-Nilan Corner, Colo, IA (Apr 25, 2018)

I've returned to the corner on the Lincoln Highway (traveling both east and west) since that 2009 stop but this was my first time reaching it on the Jefferson. That's it heading north beyond the big concrete sign. That sign was found on a nearby farm some years ago. Another just like it was also found but it was too badly damaged to restore. The sign is just one of many historic items and explanatory signs on the grounds the make the outside "museum" just as educational as the one inside.

Scott, me, & Sandii, Niland's Cafe, Colo, IA (Apr 25, 2018)

Along with a good night's rest at the motel, I enjoyed dinner and breakfast at the cafe. Local expert Scott Burka, who helped with many points of interest including that elusive fence post up the road, met me for breakfast, and we managed to get motel and cafe manager Sandii Kelly to take a little break and join us for a photo. Sadly, future customers will not be greeted by Sandii but things aren't all bad. After operating the motel and cafe under lease for several years, Sandii decided it was time for a break. She left near the end of 2018 and the cafe briefly sat idle. At the time of writing, enthusiastic new operators had just reopened the cafe so things appear to be hopping in Colo once again.

With the Lincoln Highway in tow, I headed west on the Jefferson Highway then turned south to follow it through Nevada and onto Des Moines. The JH runs right by the gold domed state capitol and provides a pretty good view of downtown De Moines without actually going through the most central part.

I entered Colo on US 65 but we parted ways when I turned west toward Nevada and US 65 continued south. The JH and US 65 get back together at the south edge of Des Moines.

Hastie Station, Carlisle, IA (Apr 25, 2018)

About two miles south of the rejoining and just a few miles from the capitol, a much smaller but equally solid looking building sits on the west side of the road. Built as a Standard Oil station by Ross Hastie, it opened in 1933, closed in 1943, and has been vacant ever since. In recent years local preservationists have worked to restore the station.

Three miles beyond the station, I turned on to Summerset Road to look at what is believed to be part of an original Jefferson Highway alignment. The unpaved road is currently identified as 138th Street. I found no dates on the wooden decked bridge but it looks like it has been there long enough to have carried the Jefferson.

Bridge on 138th St, Summerset, IA (Apr 25, 2018)

National Balloon Museum, Indianola, IA (Apr 25, 2018)

The National Balloon Museum really doesn't have much of a connection with the Jefferson Highway other than sitting beside where it once ran. Nonetheless, it makes a very interesting stop on the north side of Indianola. Unknown to me, Iowa is a great place for flying hot air balloons and Indianola has hosted many major races over the years. In 1973, the Balloon Federation of America established the museum here and moved in their headquarters. You can't get many inflated balloons inside a museum, but you can get a lot of gondolas and other historic artifacts along with loads of pictures and other informative displays. It's a great place to spend a little time.

Nearly twenty miles before rejoining US 65 south of Des Moines, I had hooked up with US 69. The two run together through Indianola then split about five miles south of town. At the split, I stayed with 69. Much of the Jefferson Highway's route from here to Texas has been taken over by US 69 and the two of us would see quite a bit of each other in the coming days.

This particular day would end in Osceola at a nice little motel about a quarter mile off of the Jefferson Highway. The Evergreen Inn accommodates its owner's full time job with a 4:00 PM check in time. That's not a problem at all for anyone paying attention and was only a slight inconvenience for me who wasn't. I simply got to look over the town a little more before settling down in a very comfortable room.

1905 decagonal barn near Leon, IA (Apr 26, 2018)

In the morning I had a wonderful breakfast at a place called Nana Greer's Family Table Restaurant. It's maybe a mile off of the Jefferson Highway and housed in a modern building but was otherwise exactly what I look for. The tasty and ample food was prepared and served by some of the nicest "nanas" I've ever met although I can't say whether or not Mrs. Greer was among them.

I then returned to US 69/Jefferson Highway and continued south. I paused briefly to photograph a 1905 ten-sided (I had to look up decagonal.) barn that Scott had described to me back at Niland's Cafe. It's about three miles north of Leon.

Downtown park, Leon, IA (Apr 26, 2018)

A small downtown park offers proof that the town of Leon is proud of its history and its place on the Jefferson Highway. The stone Jefferson Highway monument is rather new. It was dedicated in April, 2016. Some of the attention it has received is due to its spelling of the city at the highway's northern end. The city itself uses an 'i' (Winnipeg); The monument has an 'e' (Winnepeg). It isn't the first time the alternate spelling has been used, and I predict that the way Leon did it will bring in more attention than if they had gone strictly by the book.

Sally the elephant is not new but she has spent most of her time in Leon as an attention getter for the local Dairy Queen. When the DQ closed, adoring fans saved Sally and moved her to her current home where she gets attention for the whole town. Sally celebrates special occasions with appropriate accessories but I happened to catch her between holidays and unadorned.

JH striped pole, Davis City, IA (Apr 26, 2018)

It seemed to me that almost all of the small Iowan towns on the Jefferson Highway are very proud of it. Poles marked as they were during the highway's heyday are fairly common and sure help with staying on course. The one pictured indicates a left-hand turn at the north edge of Davis City.

The town of Lamoni is just three miles from the Missouri line. A huge Jefferson Highway mural on the side of a downtown building makes a nice introduction to Iowa's piece of the historic highway for those headed north. For me, it provided a nice way to remember the state as I headed to the border.

5. Iowa

JH mural, Lamoni, IA (Apr 26, 2018)

6.   Missouri

Eagleville, the first town reached in Missouri, had been bypassed by the railroads, and was determined not to have the same thing happen with the Jefferson Highway. The town's efforts included welcoming JH officials with some pretty fancy events in the park at the center of town.

Downtown park, Eagleville, MO (Apr 26, 2018)

Although the town's commercial center is now two blocks to the west on a paved US 69, the park is still there, encircled by the gravel original Jefferson Highway alignment.

Missouri had its share of unpaved Jefferson Highway, but it didn't have the most or the best or the worst. It did have some, like the graveled street around Eagleville's town square, that was quite interesting, and it had some very interesting paved JH as well. There is a drivable section about a mile south of Eagleville.

Bypassed JH south of Eagleville, MO (Apr 26, 2018)

I think this might have originally been one lane wide but I'm far from certain. I thought the pavement on the two lanes looked slightly different but I might have imagined that. Even if the difference is real, it could be the result of two contractors laying the concrete a few days, rather than years, apart. But whether the road began life with one or two lanes, it's pretty much a one-laner now. A lack of traffic has allowed grass to creep over one of the lanes in many spots.

It often happens that when a road is improved and straightened, segments of the old road survive and may end up crisscrossing the new road. That is the case here. I drove more of the bypassed concrete road, but missed out on one section, and probably should consider that a bit of good luck.

Tuggle Hill near Eagleville, MO (Apr 26, 2018)

Although I did not know its name at the time, that section was part of Tuggle Hill. I caught it from the corner of my eye and thought it looked drivable and extremely interesting. By the time I was able to turn around, I had passed the other end of the segment and my eagerness to take it on had been seriously dampened by seeing the chained gate there. I went back for a picture but I did not try driving it.

I had seen the name Tuggle Hill in my reading but didn't make the connection until I reached Saint Joseph and spoke with other conference attendees about the really cool old road segments I had seen. In two days, experts on the conference bus tour would nail down the hill's identity. Climbing this hill was a real challenge to most cars of the 1910s and '20s and Tuggle Hill appeared as a villain in many early Jefferson Highway stories until it was eventually bypassed.

I had heard of Jensen Fabrication from other travelers and had seen a few photos. I was on the lookout for the collection of scrap metal sculptures near Stanberry but that doesn't mean I was prepared.

Jensen Fabrication, Stanberry, MO (Apr 26, 2018)

In fact I was definitely not prepared for the number and variety of sculptures that Mark Jensen has created and has displayed in front of his business. The picture I've included won't prepare you, either. It shows just a fraction of the mostly whimsical pieces of art that Mark's skill and imagination have produced.

I made one more stop before reaching the conference site in Saint Joseph. Near King City, the grounds of the Tri-County Alternative Energy Education Center display several energy related items. A bridge painted with Jefferson Highway colors and logo is next to the entrance. The items displayed include a pair of huge turbine blades, that let visitors see just how big those things are, and a relocated gas station resembling a giant pump.

Energy Education Center, King City, MO (Apr 26, 2018)

I ended the day in Saint Joseph at the host hotel for the conference. This would be my third Jefferson Highway Association conference plus I've attended several events associated with other historic roads. They are almost always part of a road trip. To be honest, they are usually the reason (or excuse) for a road trip. By their very nature, they tend to be near the midpoint of the trip. Sometimes I'll meander quite a bit getting to the conference, or tack on sightseeing or personal visits following the visit, but the default action is to turn around and head home.

Saint Joseph was near the midpoint of my trip, but I would not be turning around and heading home from there. It was also near the midpoint of the Jefferson Highway which I had set out to drive end to end. Its central position was one of the reasons the Jefferson Highway Association moved its headquarters there from Des Moines in 1918. The centennial of the move was one of the things celebrated during the conference.

At least as important as its central location on the Jefferson Highway was Saint Joseph's location on another major named auto trail, the Pikes Peak – Ocean to Ocean Highway. The move allowed JH general manager J.D. Clarkson to also become general manager of the PP-OO and for the two organizations to share a building. The crossing of these two major auto trails here and at another alignment thirty some miles to the east, does provide fuel for another auto trail era Crossroads of America claim, but my vote still goes to Colo, Iowa, because of the Lincoln Highway's greater success and fame.

When I reached Saint Joseph, I had been following the Jefferson Highway for seven days and had racked up 1,026 miles. I would follow it for another eight days and 1250 miles when I moved on. It wasn't quite halfway, but it was pretty close.

In my experience, historic road conferences are breaks from the normal requirements of traveling but they can't really be called relaxing. The physical efforts of driving and looking for food and lodging are replaced by attempts to absorb information from presentations or check out points of interest on tours. It's not stressful. It's wonderfully rewarding which is why we do it, but it is rarely relaxing in the same way laying by a pool is relaxing.

I spent three nights and two days in Saint Joseph. The first day was presentation day. It began with the proclamation of Jefferson Highway Recognition Day by Saint Joseph's mayor, Darrell McMurry, and proceeded with presentations on local history, stories of the road, and reports on the association. I succumbed to gentle pressure and stumbled through a short talk on the drive I was in the middle of.

A bus tour filled the second day. It headed north from Saint Joseph along the route I had followed two days earlier.

Local experts pointed out bits of roadside history as we passed them. Stops at the Energy Education Center near King City and at Jensen Fabrication near Stanberry were repeats for me, but I enjoyed them and managed to learn an additional thing or two. The bus tour confirmed that the bypassed road I had been so impressed with really was Tuggle Hill.

I got to see some new things on the way back. Two alignments of the road exist south of Bethany, and the tour followed the "other one" as it traveled south. This route goes through the town of Cameron and was known as the "Cameron Cut Off". Pieces of an older alignment and other points of interest were identified as we passed. The Cameron Depot Museum, where we stopped, contains a Jefferson Highway display along with lots of local history.

JHA Conference attendees, Cameron, MO (Apr 28, 2018)

I realize that pictures from the conference might be conspicuous by their absence. Photos of people making presentations and giving speeches aren't generally of much interest to anyone not associated with the event, and the tour's main stops were at places photographed earlier on my own drive to Saint Joseph. An exception to that was the museum in Cameron. I've included a picture of the museum, and am using it to prove that I – and a bunch of other people – really were at the conference.

We left the "Cut Off" branch of the Jefferson Highway in Cameron. In fact, we left the Jefferson Highway entirely and headed back to Saint Joseph more or less on that other cross-country auto trail that was once headquartered with the Jefferson, the Pikes Peak – Ocean to Ocean Highway.

THE INTERNATIONAL JEFFERSON HIGHWAY ASSOCIATION
Proudly presents the
AMBASSADOR AWARD
TO
DENNIS GIBSON
FOR HIS "END-TO-END" DRIVE
ON THE HISTORIC JEFFERSON HIGHWAY
"From Pine to Palm"

Presented at the Seventh Annual Conference of
The Jefferson Highway Association
St. Joseph, Missouri---April 28, 2018

President

JHA Ambassador Award, St Joseph (Apr 28, 2018)

Back in Saint Joseph, I obtained further proof of my attendance during the awards banquet that followed the bus tour. I wasn't too far from the podium and taking pictures of some of the award recipients when I heard my own name. When I learned that I was being presented with an Ambassador Award for my end-to-end drive, I protested. I pointed out that I'd so far covered less than half of the highway's length. But president Glenn Smith expressed confidence that I would make it and pointed out that I was now obligated to do so. I appreciated the award and the confidence, and I'm sure glad I reached the southern terminus and didn't have to give it back.

In the morning, I said goodbye to the good folks of the JHA and set out to complete that end-to-end drive. Even though I knew that the building was long gone, I made a point of looking over the intersection where the combined JH and PP-OO headquarters once stood.

MO-Z east of Dearborn, MO (Apr 29, 2018)

Saint Joseph is not a huge city and it did not take terribly long to get beyond its limits. I was soon passing through small towns like Faucett and Dearborn and the spaces in between. It felt good to be back on the open road in my own car.

Kansas City, MO (Apr 29, 2018)

The "Cut Off" route that was part way of the bus tour, reconnects with the main Jefferson Highway alignment in Trimble. Construction blocked my route in Smithville which put me on US 169 a little earlier than intended. I exited the divided highway at Nashua as planned, and proceeded to Kansas City on wide city streets. Following the Jefferson Highway spared me any serious traffic congestion in the city center, but kept me on semi-busy streets passing through built up areas for quite some time. Three different alignments of the Jefferson Highway leave Kansas City headed south. I followed the easternmost alignment, and my memory is that open countryside did not reappear until well past Lee's Summit on MO 291. Between Harrisonville, which has some nice murals depicting local history, and Archie, the Jefferson Highway is now a frontage road alongside I-49. I-49 and the Jefferson Highway will travel together for the rest of the day. For the most part, the two are just neighbors, but there are spots where the old road is buried under the new.

CR 1001 south of Archie, MO (Apr 29, 2018)

At Archie, the JH gets to move away from I-49 for a few miles. When it moves back, it climbs onto the expressway. Before that happened, I was treated to one of my favorite views of the trip. The route follows MO AA for a very short distance then leaves it to pass through a canopy of trees on an unpaved county road. When the scene first entered my vision, I imagined that elves and fairies would be waiting just beyond. The truth is that Crescent Hill Cemetery is just ahead on the left.

CR 2255, Bates County, MO (Apr 29, 2018)

The Jefferson Highway rejoins I-49 at Adrian, but leaves it just a few miles later at Passaic. In rather short order, the road passes under the interstate and through the town of Butler. Although I didn't know it at the time, at Butler's south edge, I entered territory not yet visited by Google Street View. That's not always a sign of cool stuff ahead, but it worked out here. I was soon on gravel and a particularly long and straight stretch caught my eye. Why arrow straight roads that disappear into the distance appeal to me about as much as winding roads with visibility measured in yards is a mystery, but not one I'm working to solve.

Although it is never more than a couple of miles from the expressway, the road has a slightly isolated feel. It passes quite close to the Ripgut Prairie Natural Area so maybe some of that natural feeling just leaks out. There is almost no traffic. This allowed me to walk around, without getting run over, attempting, without much success, to photograph the remnants of a Marais des Cygnes River bridge that were partly visible through trees along the banks.

Beaver dam near Rich Hill, MO (Apr 29, 2018)

After asphalt replaces the gravel, the road crosses over the expressway and runs beside it for about a mile before moving to the west. It was here that I passed a beaver dam just yards from the road.

Old US 71 bridge over Marmaton River, MO (Apr 29, 2018)

The Jefferson Highway enters I-49 at the next interchange and exits at the one after that to follow a bit of Old US 71. It crosses the Marmaton River on a 1925 through truss bridge. Not only did the bridge catch my eye, so did the unusual solid rock river bank. Following another brief stint on the expressway, the JH exits to enter the town of Nevada.

Nevada was a town I'd been looking forward to reaching. There are interesting buildings, such as the old Vernon County Jail (now Bushwhacker Museum) and an impressive courthouse, right on the Jefferson Highway, but the building I was targeting is a block from the route.

White Grill, Nevada, MO (Apr 29, 2018)

I'd only recently learned of the eighty year old White Grill and its reputation for outstanding 'burgers, and I was ready to see if I agreed. To cut to the chase, I most certainly did. As is my habit, I sat at the counter and watched my meal being prepared. I could have dined in one of booths that were added earlier this century, or in my car. Curb service is available and operates the old fashioned way: honk your horn.

I watched big balls of fresh ground beef get smashed flat on the grill and buckets of Suzy Qs being deep fried. One of those balls and a generous portion of those Suzy Qs were mine. I was definitely the only person in Nevada and maybe in all of Missouri who did not know what Suzy Qs are. Many restaurants now serve them but this is where they were invented. The White Grill's founder, Red McLaughlin, is credited with developing the spiral cut potatoes that are kept in water until being cooked. They resemble fast food curly fries about as much as fresh cut Montgomery Inn Saratoga chips resemble Pringles.

I did have to get onto I-49 for two three mile long segments but the bulk of the twenty-five miles between Nevada and Lamar was on narrow side roads, some paved, some not. In Lamar I took an unplanned side trip.

Salvaged JH bridge, Lamar, MO (Apr 29, 2018)

As I turned a corner to head into downtown Lamar, one of the two men standing near the street motioned for me to stop. It was Joe Davis, a researcher at the Barton County Historical Society. He had spotted the Jefferson Highway magnets still firmly attached to my car doors and wanted to say hi. We chatted about my in process trip, the recent conference, and some local history. At some point he asked if I wanted to see a bridge. Not just any bridge, of course, this was a retired Jefferson Highway bridge.

I was basically following the original Jefferson Highway alignment as best I could. Two other alignments reportedly had also entered Lamar from the north although details are not clear. All crossed the North Fork of the Spring River at some point. I had just followed the westernmost alignment over the river on 12th Street using a modern bridge. The easternmost alignment, which may have been the last of the three, is also still in use and its 1925 bridge had been replaced in 2003. Most bridges are either demolished or bypassed and blocked when they are retired, but this one had been moved to a nearby field. Joe gave me directions, I drove to the field, and that's why I have a picture of a Jefferson Highway bridge that is touching neither road nor river.

As is well known, Harry Truman was born in Lamar, and his birthplace still stands. It is about a block off of the easternmost JH alignment.

At grade crossing south of Lamar, MO (Apr 29, 2018)

A single Jefferson Highway alignment runs south out of Lamar. I've included a "something you don't see every day" picture from the drive between Lamar and Jasper. The train and truck reveal the recent date of the photo, but without them the photo could be mistaken for one taken 50, 60, or many more years ago. The road is gravel, there are no automatic gates or flashing lights at the crossing, and it is at grade.

Although at grade crossings, where trains and automobiles pass through the same space, have not been completely eliminated, they have been reduced considerably. Crossings of this sort were among the biggest dangers faced by early motorists, and the majority have been eliminated with overpasses, underpasses, and rerouting. Most that remain are guarded by automatic gates and other warning devices. Here the crossing continues to look much as it did when an active Jefferson Highway used it. Few are exposed to the risk, however, since the main traffic flow was moved a mile west to US 71/I-49.

Police Department, Jasper, MO (Apr 29, 2018)

Reaching Jasper put me back in semi-familiar territory. The town lies at the northern edge of the county of the same name. The 2016 Jefferson Highway Association conference was held in Carthage, the county seat, and online conference related information included driving instructions for the Jefferson Highway in Jasper County. I had taken advantage of those instructions and traveled the JH from Jasper to my motel in Carthage. I would be back there tonight.

Boots Court, Carthage, MO (Apr 29, 2018)

The wonderfully restored Boots Court is one of my favorite places to stay. It really is possible to think you've stepped back in time here. Every room has a radio. There are no TVs. When you first enter your room, the radio will probably be on and playing 1940s music from a local station. Indications that you haven't actually entered the 1940s are limited to invisible, but appreciated, WiFi and air conditioning.

The motel's architectural neon was restored shortly before my 2016 stay. A storm damaged it shortly before this one. The dark section to the right of the vacancy sign had yet to be repaired. Although they are nearly impossible to see, the picture includes co-owner Debye Harvey and onsite manager Debbie Dee sitting in front of the motel.

Lowell Davis, me, and Debbie Dee, Carthage, MO (Apr 30, 2018)

In the morning, Debbie Dee agreed to join me for breakfast and we walked the short distance down the street to the Pancake Hut. Before we finished, local artist Lowell Davis walked in and Debbie invited him to join us. Davis is, among other accomplishments, the creator of Red Oak II, and we had been discussing a visit to the whimsical village along with checking out several new pieces of his work around town. The visit did happen after getting a picture with Davis and one of his art installations in front of the restaurant.

Carthage businesses sometimes use the Crossroads of America label for their city. Their claim does not involve the Jefferson Highway. It comes from the period of US Numbered Highways and is based on the crossing of US 71 and US 66. US 71 now bypasses the town, and US 66 has been decommissioned. Being decommissioned hasn't prevented – and probably helped – Historic Route 66 becoming possibly the most popular route for heritage travel in the world. It has carried me through Carthage many times.

In fact, leaving Carthage on the Jefferson Highway is something of a first for me. The Jefferson Highway and Historic Route 66 followed similar but not identical paths between Carthage and the Kansas border. They share a street as they exit Carthage. I departed Boots Court on a course I've followed multiple times in the past but this time it's called the Jefferson Highway.

7.   Kansas

The Jefferson Highway alignment I'm following enters Kansas in conjunction with Historic Route 66 but they quickly diverge. The railroad overpass at the left of this chapter's first photo once carried US 66 and is often associated with entering Kansas on the historic highway. The 1922 overpass was almost brand new when US 66 and the other US Numbered Highways came into being. The Jefferson Highway enters Galena on Clark Street.

Clark St, Galena, KS (Apr 30, 2018)

Galena, KS (Apr 30, 2018)

The Jefferson Highway turns left on Main Street and quickly rejoins Historic Route 66 in front of Cars on the Route, a popular Route 66 themed business. I've been through this intersection many times, but never from this direction, and I was quite surprised to see the ghost sign filled wall on the building across the street.

Although the JH alignment I'm following cuts across the southeast corner of Kansas much like US 66 once did, the two roads share nothing outside of Galena. US 66 turns west at 7th Street and enters Oklahoma after spending 13 miles in Kansas. The Jefferson Highway turns west on 10th street and enters Oklahoma after spending 17.5 miles in Kansas.

Schermerhorn Rd/Pierce St, Galena, KS (Apr 30, 2018)

5.9 of those 17.5 Kansas miles were unpaved. I encountered the first unpaved section when I turned onto Schermerhorn Road at the edge of Galena. It continued as the Jefferson Highway curved onto Pierce Street.

Federal-Aid Secondary Highway 1178, Lowell, KS (Apr 30, 2018)

Some of the paved roads offered interesting names along with interesting visuals. For example, there is the narrow Federal-Aid Secondary Highway 1178 bordered by patches of water as it approaches Lowell Reservoir.

Monument to Reese, KS (Apr 30, 2018)

Both the asphalt and gravel roads I traveled were well maintained, and, when that's the case, it doesn't take long to cover less than twenty miles regardless of what sort of surface you are driving on. I was at the Oklahoma border about half an hour after leaving Galena. A marker stands on the Kansas side of the border that is essentially a tombstone for a town.

The town of Treece, with a 2010 population of 138, once stood about a half mile west of the marker. Founded in 1917, it was part of the tri-state mining district that supplied much of the lead and zinc used in both world wars. The severe risks of mine shaft cave-ins and lead contaminated mounds of chat were eventually recognized and a US government buyout was authorized in 2010. Residents were relocated and the town's buildings leveled. On May 9, 2012, the town of Treece was officially dissolved.

8.   Oklahoma

This would be my second drive of the Jefferson Highway through Oklahoma. The first JHA conference I ever attended was in Muskogee in 2015. It's a real stretch to say that Muskogee is in the middle of the state, but I pulled off a miniature version of the current full length drive by wrapping a drive of all of Oklahoma's Jefferson Highway around that conference. I had connected with the JH at the Treece monument, and strayed away from it after crossing the Texas border.

This would actually be my third visit to Picher, the first town south of the Kansas-Oklahoma line. In addition to the 2015 visit, I'd driven through the town as a Historic Route 66 side trip in 2010. Picher was also part of the tri-state mining district, and, like Treece, Kansas, has suffered irreparably for it. Although once much larger than Treece, its 2000 population of 1,640 had plummeted to just 20 in 2010.

Obviously, Picher was essentially a ghost town when I first visited. That was in June of 2010, and the town had been dis-incorporated on September first the year before. But there had been quite a few buildings standing then. Several remained in 2015, but in 2018 the majority had been flattened.

Picher, OK (Apr 30, 2018)

Oddly, a couple of the buildings that remained were actually in use. One was the district road maintenance building; The other housed local police. I pulled off of the main road and drove around a residential area. With most buildings gone, I imagine it's rather difficult to not notice someone driving around for any length of time. Eventually an officer did approach me but it wasn't even slightly confrontational. A friendly chat, a few more pictures, and I was on my way.

The town of Commerce, home of Mickey Mantle, felt kind of familiar not only because of that 2015 JH drive but because of several Historic Route 66 drives. Same with Miami with the last operating Ku-Ku drive-in and the glorious Coleman Theater. South of Miami, the JH turns west and I covered some gravel driving through the towns of Welch and Bluejacket. In Vinita, I ventured a block off of the JH for dinner at the famous Clanton's Cafe. Vinita is also where I spent the night.

Railroad underpass south of Adair, OK (May 1, 2018)

The path of the Jefferson Highway south of Vinita has pretty much been taken over and streamlined by US 69, but many paved and unpaved segments are still around. You might think the photo of the railroad underpass was taken in the 1920s until you notice the modern graffiti.

Double drinking fountain in Wagoner, OK (May 1, 2018)

One bowl of this unusual drinking fountain in downtown Wagoner supplied city water and the other germicidal water. The high salt content of the germicidal water reportedly rusted out the fountain prematurely.

Collapsed bridge at OKay, OK (May 1, 2018)

Having driven the Jefferson Highway through here in 2015, I knew of a few points of interest but local JH experts Glenn Smith and Roger Bell turned me onto some I'd have otherwise missed. One was a partially collapsed bridge over an old channel of the Verdigris River in the town of Okay. It's not easy to see, but there is a metal through truss span at the top of the picture. The wooden deck on this side of the span has collapsed on the near end and is now angled up sharply to the standing part of the bridge.

Back in chapter 6 there is a picture of a bridge near Lamar, Missouri, that was moved away from the river it once crossed. Here we have a case of the river moving away from the bridge. To be honest, water still flows under the 1925 bridge but the river's main channel was moved about a quarter-mile west in the late 1960s as part of the McClellan Kerr Navigation project. It was this project that made the Tulsa Port of Catoosa possible. A replacement bridge was built about half a mile downstream.

Abandoned bridge near Muskogee, OK (May 1, 2018)

There is another abandoned Jefferson Highway bridge a few miles farther south. This one crossed the Arkansas river, and it's one I was already aware of. A bus tour at the 2015 JHA conference made a stop at the bridge, and participants were able to walk to and on the 1922 bridge. It was retired around 1980.

With Roger Bell at Club Lunch, Muskogee, OK (May 1, 2018)

In Muskogee, I hooked up with one of the fellows providing me with inside information on the area. Roger Bell and I met for lunch at a 115 year old restaurant. Although there have been a few name and owner changes over the years, some sort of eating establishment has operated here since 1913. It stayed in the same family through the most recent ownership change when Cindy Littrell bought the restaurant from her parents who had operated the place since 1982. In addition to making me better informed, Roger made me an Honorary Okie from Muskogee with a new hat to prove it.

During the four days of the 2015 JHA conference, I had visited most if not all of the JH related sites in Muskogee. As a consequence, I did not seek out many of them on this trip although I did snap some not so good drive-by pictures of places like Spaulding Park and the restored 1925 Conoco station where the JH turns south on 24th street.

JH mileage sign, Muskogee, OK (Apr 30, 2015)

The 2015 conference included a ribbon cutting beneath a sign post that had been filled just days before. I've included a picture of the sign taken that day. It has become quite an important Jefferson Highway landmark in Muskogee.

Bypassed JH south of Muskogee, OK (May 1, 2018)

Bypassed JH south of Muskogee, OK (May 1, 2018)

About a half mile south of the Muskogee city limits, the original route of the Jefferson Highway is now on private land. In 2015, our tour bus stopped there so we could stand at the gate blocking it and look at the road beyond. I did my own stop and look two days later when I passed the point as I continued my drive of the JH in Oklahoma. Today I got to drive some of what I had only gazed at before.

I did not crash through a gate or charge past a wall of "No Trespassing" signs. In fact, while I did drive beyond where the gate was in 2015, I did so in the belief that it was OK with the owner, and I turned around when I saw a "Posted" sign. There had been talk at the conference about the gate being absent and I asked Roger about it over lunch. He had spoken with the land owner who said he did intend to eventually replace the gate, but that he wasn't in any real hurry to do so. I took that as an indication that it was probably alright for an old man with JH magnets on his car to take a look. The road is probably close to a mile in length but I drove only about half a mile before encountering the sign and turning back.

Muffler Man near Summit, OK (May 1, 2018)

Modern US 69 is used to reach the next bit of old Jefferson Highway alignment near the town of Summit. An only slightly repurposed muffler man guards the remnants of some rather classic cars just a few miles south of Summit. Although there is no muffler, that could be a length of exhaust pipe he holds while looking over an immobile fleet that includes an early '60s Falcon Ranchero, a 1960 Chevy sedan, and several Mustangs.

The town of Checotah is just over ten miles south of the muffler man and his rusting buddies. There's a lot of rodeo history in the area and that's just one of the things displayed at Checotah's Heartland Heritage Center Museum and Gallery. Checotah's pride in being on the Jefferson Highway is evident in a marker at the north edge of town.

Jefferson Highway sign, Checotah, OK (May 1, 2018)

Leak's Garage, Crowder, OK (May 1, 2018)

In the twenty some miles between Muskogee and Lake Eufaula, the Jefferson Highway and US 69 cross each other a few times, but the old road is forced to join the new road to cross over the lake. Lake Eufaula was created in 1964 by the damming of the Canadian River. Like most lakes made by humans using rivers, Lake Eufaula twists and turns a bit and has a number of fingers. Those twists, turns, and fingers mean that not all of the old road is buried beneath the water. Several pieces, including one through the town of Eufaula, can be driven. The old road can also be driven into, but not through, the town of Crowder.

Ghost sign in McAlester, OK (May 1, 2018)

Once south of the lake, it is possible to leave the US 69 of today to pick up the Jefferson Highway and enter the town of McAlester. The JH is signed as US 69 Business through McAlester.

J. J. McAlester served in the Confederate Army then founded The J. J. McAlester Mercantile Company around which the town of McAlester sort of grew. His marriage to Rebecca Burney, a Chickasaw, enabled him to do business in Indian Territory. He also operated several coal mines in the area and eventually became Oklahoma's second Lieutenant Governor. The mostly Italian miners received much of their pay in scrip redeemable only at the company store. I'm guessing that the building bearing the big ghost sign is where that scrip was used.

Old gas stations on Jefferson Highway, McAlester, OK (May 1, 2018)

The outstanding ghost sign is hardly the only thing making McAlester interesting. The town also contains three restored gas stations. The Jefferson Highway runs right between a Conoco and a Phillip's 66 station. A 1935 Texaco station is just a few blocks away.

I spent the night in McAlester in a spot almost but not quite on the Jefferson Highway. I went a little farther off of the route for one of the best meals of the trip. The meal was at Pete's Place in the town of Krebs, a McAlester suburb. Not only does Pete's serve great food, it's where regional favorite Choc Beer is brewed.

Overall, I was quite happy with the motel, too. It is independently owned, reasonably priced, very clean and comfortable, and clearly convenient. A clue to the decor is in the name: Happy Days Hotel. The parking spaces are marked in pink. The walls are lined with records and pictures of James Dean and the like. The breakfast room is chrome and Formica on black and white tile. I didn't actually make it there for breakfast but walked next door to Angel's Diner. There I found more black and white tile flooring with pink and turquoise walls holding more pictures of James and Elvis and Marilyn.

Angel's Diner, McAlester, OK (May 2, 2018)

Food and service were both quite good and, although I'm not really a fan of the Elvis and Marilyn decor, I'm OK with it. There is one item, however, that frequently shows up in businesses of this sort that I find a bit irritating while simultaneously understanding exactly why it's there. It was present at Angel's. Just inside the door a big Route 66 shield was attached to a large black trash can.

I'm a pretty big fan of Route 66. I understand that it has become a symbol of road trips and fun diners and "happy days". I also understand that Route 66 themed items are the most readily available road related decorations that exist. But it has become something of a pet peeve of mine to find an establishment on or near a historic highway casually promoting Route 66 while being completely oblivious to the historic road right outside their door. To be fair, I can't really say whether or not the people at Angel's Diner and Happy Days Hotel are oblivious to the nearby Jefferson Highway but I didn't spot any JH signs.

Bridge on Old Highway 69, Savanna, OK (May 2, 2018)

Leaving McAlester involved a few miles of divided US 69 before I could slip off on some good old two-lane to drive through Savanna. Then it was back to the wide road for several miles. I would exit and reenter US 69 five more times before hitting the long stretch of old road that would take me almost to Texas.

Rock outcropping near Limestone Gap, OK (May 2, 2018)

The third of those departures was onto Chockie Mountain Road. It was an interesting enough road but the only thing that really caught my eye was a rock outcropping off to the right just before it merged back into US 69. It's not very big. The west is full of rock faces that make this one look tiny and even places like Kentucky and Tennessee have countless exposed rocks bigger than this one. It isn't even particularly interesting looking or oddly shaped. What caught my attention was that it seemed alone and out of place.

As I was writing this, I became curious about the rock formation and the road it was on. Was there a mountain nearby? Maybe one where someone named Chockie once lived? As ludicrous as it sounds, I even wondered if the rock itself was named Chockie Mountain. I never did find Chockie Mountain on a map, but I found an article that described it as a long narrow ridge. Maybe it's what the maps I've seen identify as Limestone Ridge or maybe it's something else entirely. That same article indicated that this section of road was the last bit of two-lane on the primary route between

Tulsa and Dallas. I found other stuff, too, and, even though the things I found have absolutely nothing to do with the Jefferson Highway, I feel the need to share them.

Chockie is indeed a place name. Singer Reba McEntire once lived there. It is still listed on maps although it lost its post office in 1937. Prior to 1904, Chockie was only half of its name. The full name was Chickiechockie. It combined the nicknames of a pair of twin girls. The twins' parents were Charles LeFlore and Mary Guy LeFlore. Charles was a Choctaw; Mary was a Chickasaw. When the twins were born, on July 4, 1871, the names of their parents' tribes were used as their middle names. The full names were Laurina Choctaw LeFlore and Serena Chickasaw LeFlore but apparently they were known mostly by shortened versions of their middle names. When the place they lived needed a name, Chickiechockie was it.

There's an indirect connection with J. J. McAlester in the change to just Chockie. As mentioned, McAlester took a Chickasaw bride. This was not at all uncommon and both of the LeFlore twins married white men. Chockie married a fellow named Charles Maupin and moved with him to Texas. Chickie married Lee Cruce and remained in Oklahoma. Lee Cruce campaigned to be the first governor of Oklahoma when it became a state in 1907 but did not succeed. He did better the next time around and became Oklahoma's second governor in 1911. His running mate was J. J. McAlester. Chickie LeFlore Cruce died on May 6, 1903. It was Lee Cruce who requested that the town's name be changed to just Chockie on February 8, 1904.

While none of this has any connection with the Jefferson Highway, road fans do have a reason to honor one of the players. It was Governor Cruce who established the Oklahoma Department of Highways.

Mitchell Road, Stringtown, OK (May 2, 2018)

At Stringtown, Mitchell Road begins a scenic four mile stretch of old Jefferson Highway. Unpaved sections appear between sections of asphalt but it isn't clear to me whether they were never paved or whether the thin asphalt has simply broken up and disappeared over the years. I'm pretty sure that my enjoyment of this quiet and peaceful drive was enhanced just a little by the fact that I had risked my life getting to it.

The north end of Mitchell road is accessed by a short section of Wells Street. The route was programmed into my GPS so I knew exactly where the turn was as I headed south on US 69. The turn didn't surprise me; The lack of a left turn lane did. I did not consciously analyze things and decide there would be one. It was an almost instinctive expectation that a busy four-lane highway would have a lane dedicated to turning left onto a cross street. There was no such lane, plus, since this was an undivided four-lane, there was not even a little space in the median to tuck into. My turn signal was on and I was slowing but there was traffic in both lanes behind me. I touched the brakes then dashed across the prow of an oncoming semi.

OK, so maybe the semi was not actually life threateningly close and the dashing was relative (Subaru Foresters are not known for their dashability.), but it was definitely not the gentle turn to the left I had envisioned.

Phillips 66 station, Atoka, OK (May 2, 2018)

The current US 69 stays with the old Jefferson Highway through Atoka, but I briefly left it anyway. The reason was to visit a restored Phillips 66 station just a few blocks off of the historic route. Constructed in 1932, the station now houses the Atoka County Chamber of Commerce.

What is probably the longest and most picturesque section of old Jefferson Highway in Oklahoma begins at the south edge of Tushka. Modern US 69 will not be touched for the next 30+ miles. The first dozen miles, to the town of Caddo, is a mix of Portland concrete, solid asphalt, nearly disintegrated asphalt, and stretches that may have never seen asphalt. Besides the interesting variety of surfaces, the section has a nice railroad underpass, a cool 1928 through truss bridge, and a section of almost-canopy road.

1927 underpass near Tushka, OK (May 2, 2018)

1928 bridge near Caney, OK (May 2, 2018)

The railroad underpass, with the year 1927 cast into it, shows up about a half mile after departing US 69. The bridge is just a few miles farther on near the town of Caney.

Almost-canopy road near Caney, OK (May 2, 2018)

The picture of what I've called an almost-canopy road was taken a little more than half a mile beyond the bridge. There are roads in Florida where the trees touch overhead and which are officially designated "canopy roads". Here the trees don't quite form a tight canopy but it's close. Driving through areas like this feels just a little bit like driving through a tunnel.

I started this long section of old Jefferson Highway by exiting US 69 and slipping through a railroad underpass. About two miles north of Caddo, I slipped back to the west side of the tracks but it wasn't to return to US 69. The road I turned onto was Caddo Highway and it would carry me all the way to the north edge of Durant, about ten miles away. It was not a non-stop drive, however. I would checkout a bit of downtown Caddo before moving onto Durant.

Railroad underpass near Caddo, OK (May 2, 2018)

Craighead's Five and Dime, Caddo, OK (May 2, 2018)

Once inside the limits of Caddo, the highway takes on the name Main Street but that seems to be an honorary title only. The town's business district is aligned along an intersecting east-west street that was once a buffalo trail. That history is noted in silhouettes and other images of the animal displayed along the thoroughfare and in its name: Buffalo Street. Several of the buildings that line Buffalo Street are empty, but those that aren't are definitely worth a look. An enterprise on each side of the street caught my eye.

On the south side of Buffalo Street, Craighead's five and dime has been operating since 1955. It carries much of the miscellaneous items that a small town needs plus a bunch of unusual gift type items. Chatting with the proprietor was fun and I found a couple of humorous greeting cards I've not seen anywhere else.

Across the street is the Indian Territory Museum where one can learn a lot about Caddo and the surrounding area. I asked about an aerial photo of a large group of people standing in the middle of Buffalo Street. I expected to be told that it commemorated a centennial or something similar but that wasn't the case at all. One day in 2016, someone with a "cherry picker" decided the town needed a picture of itself and invited anyone who wanted to be in it to step right up. That's just the sort of town Caddo is.

Three Valley Museum, Durant, OK (May 2, 2018)

I stopped in one more Oklahoma town and that was Durant, about fifteen miles from Texas. I had been thinking of ending the day here but turned up better lodging options on the other side of the border. I headed on after checking out the Three Valley Museum.

Chickasaw Road near Colbert, OK (May 2, 2018)

The street I turned onto at the north edge of Durant was signed US 69 Business. I suspect it was once an alignment of the primary Route 69. I followed the business route through Durant until it merged with the current US 69 south of town. I would cross the Red River on US 69, but before that happened, I would exit the modern four-lane to drive some older Jefferson Highway alignments. One of those followed Chickasaw Road where I got a picture of Oklahoma clay pavement and a sky filled with clues about what tomorrow would bring.

9.   Texas

Those clouds that were waiting for me in Texas opened up during the night, and I awakened to a wet world with rain still falling. I was in Denison, Dwight Eisenhower's birthplace. I had been in Denison once before, but it was on a day when the birthplace museum was closed, and I hoped to check it out on this visit.

Eisenhower birthplace, Denison, TX (May 3, 2018)

I found the museum open and signed up for a tour of the nearby house. I drove there in the light rain and walked to the porch just as it picked up considerably. I quickly realized two things: 1) I was the only tour participant, and 2) the guide was not dry and waiting inside as I had assumed.

Rain from porch at Eisenhower birthplace, Denison, TX (May 3, 2018)

When the guide pulled up beside the house, I tried to convince him that he didn't need to brave the rain to give a tour to just me, but John splashed his way to the house, parked his umbrella at the door, and gave me a great one-on-one tour.

When the tour was over, I dawdled around Denison a little then picked up the Jefferson Highway and continued my journey. Although I was never completely free from rain, I had it pretty good. Extremely heavy rain and dangerous winds were all around me, but I seemed to be always a little ahead or a little behind the worst of it.

I don't doubt that I missed noticing some smaller points of interest because of the rain, but it also prompted me to spend more time at indoor attractions than I might have otherwise. Apparently, a real deluge had preceded my arrival at Sam Rayburn's place. Rayburn spent a total of 48 years in the US House of Representatives including 17 as Speaker. I would certainly have stopped at his home and museum in any weather but the continuing rain probably made me a little extra ready to spend time inside.

Sam Rayburn home, Bonham, TX (May 3, 2018)

Sam Rayburn's 1947 Cadillac, Bonham, TX (May 3, 2018)

Rayburn built this house a little west of Bonham in 1916, and it was his home until his death in 1961. Most of the furnishings remain as they were when he lived here. The Cadillac was a gift from fellow congressmen. As Speaker of the House, Rayburn was supplied with a government limousine. When Republicans took over the House in 1947, Sam lost his job and his car. He was elected Minority Leader and 142 Democratic congressmen chipped in $25 apiece (the largest amount Rayburn would accept as a gift) to pay for the 1947 Cadillac Fleetwood. When Rayburn brought the car back to Texas, his old garage had to be modified a little to accommodate it.

Sam Rayburn Library, Bonham, TX (May 3, 2018)

There is no doubt that Sam Rayburn conducted a little business at the house west of Bonham, but the focus there is primarily on his personal life. Inside the town, his political career gets the focus at the Sam Rayburn Library. Rayburn was in congress while eight different men served as president and his seventeen years as Speaker of the House is a record.

Inside the library is the marble rostrum that stood in the U.S. House of Representatives from 1857 to 1950 and which Sam must have pounded on more than anybody else.

From the time it left Kansas until it entered Texas, the Jefferson Highway followed a generally southwest course. At Denison, it took on a southeast heading directed at New Orleans, Louisiana. The path through Oklahoma was fairly straight. The southeast course through Texas was accomplished with some pretty big stair-steps. From Denison to Bonham it was more east than south. In Bonham it turned to the south to reach Greenville. Here the stair-steps became even more pronounced with the route heading almost due east to Mount Pleasant, due south to Gladewater, then east again to Shreveport, Louisiana. The town of Sulphur Springs lies near the midpoint of that east-west line between Greenville and Mount Pleasant.

Crosswalk sign, Sulphur Springs, TX (May 3, 2018)

Although I can't recall where it came from, I've long accepted as absolute truth the saying "Life is too serious a matter to be taken seriously". Sulphur Springs seems to believe that, too. Beside the gorgeous Hopkins County courthouse is an impressive veterans area with an array of stone monuments and a good looking plaza with fountains and flowers. The downtown streets are clean and – even in the light rain – attractive. Inviting eateries and other businesses are nearby. This is clearly a town justifiably proud of itself, but, at the same time, not taking itself too seriously as evident from the Ministry of Silly Walks image on the crosswalk sign.

Hopkins County courthouse, Sulphur Springs, TX (May 4, 2018)

Public restroom, Sulphur Springs, TX (May 3, 2018)

The city's playful spirit is also apparent in the unique public restrooms on the aforementioned plaza. Through the magic of one-way glass walls, these can be used in complete privacy while viewing those fountains, the courthouse, and anonymous passersby.

1935 underpass, Mount Vernon, TX (May 4, 2018)

I spent the night near Sulphur Springs then continued on in the morning. So did the rain. The rain did limit my outside-the-car activity but it didn't keep me from photographing water on the windshield and the occasional background underpass.

Between Greenville and Mount Vernon the route was primarily on old or current US 67. At Mount Vernon I dropped a bit to the south and picked up a frontage road on the south side of I-30. I turned south in Mount Pleasant to follow US 271 all the way to Gladewater. From there the route was centered around US 80 to the Louisiana border. I did spend most of those miles on the US route but there were quite a few opportunities to slip off of it and follow some older alignments, too.

East of Hallsville, TX (May 4, 2018)

One of the coolest of these was on a narrow tree lined county road just a couple miles east of Hallsville, and I'm sure it was even cooler without a wet windshield in the way.

Harrison County Courthouse, Marshall, TX (May 4, 2018)

In Marshall, the Jefferson Highway goes right past the Harrison County Courthouse which is a worthy competitor of the one in Sulphur Springs for the title of best looking courthouse in Texas.

About halfway between Marshall and where US 80 merges with I-20, the Jefferson Highway leaves the US route and travels a bit to the north on two-lane Farm to Market roads. The JH and US 80 reconnect briefly when the latter leaves I-20, but they will split and rejoin one more time before exiting Texas.

Waskom Ave, Waskom, TX (May 4, 2018)

That last split was inside the town of Waskom, and put me on some narrow heavily-patched road that looked a lot more isolated than it was. Louisiana was less than a mile and a half beyond where I rejoined US 80.

10. Louisiana

I entered the seventh and final Jefferson Highway state on US 80, and quickly went to roost at a chain motel less than ten miles from the Texas-Louisiana line. As described earlier, the general direction of the route from Denison, Texas, to New Orleans is southeast with some sizable stair-steps in eastern Texas. Those steps do not end cleanly at the state line. In fact, one of the sharpest is at Shreveport. The road approaches the city on an almost due east course from Gladewater, Texas, then heads almost due south to the town of Keithville on US-171. There is some uncertainty about route details here but it seems likely that the original Jefferson Highway reached downtown Shreveport on what was essentially a spur. My own route deviated from the true JH with a path that never quite reached the city center.

The two old maps reproduced in this book's first chapter make it look like the road between Shreveport and New Orleans was almost a straight line. While it is true that there are no more giant stair-steps like those that defined the route in Texas, a straight line it is not.

With one delightful exception, the divided four-lane of US 171 carries the Jefferson Highway all the way to Mansfield. That exception is in the town of Stonewall. The surviving older alignment is signed Old Jefferson Road, and is lined with trees much as it might have been in the 1920s.

It's probably about the same width, too. The biggest indicator that this is not the 1920s is the smooth modern asphalt surface.

Old Jefferson Road, Stonewall, LA (May 5, 2018)

Old Jefferson Highway, Mansfield, LA (May 5, 2018)

At Mansfield, US 171 heads straight south. The Jefferson Highway splits off and eventually leaves town on LA 175 to maintain its southeast direction. On its way through town, it spends a little time on a street that still carries the Jefferson Highway name.

The Jefferson Highway abandons LA 175 in Belmont, and makes its way to Natchitoches on a couple of other state highways. Its route through the city includes the historic section on the banks of the Cane River but I didn't get to drive that initially. When I arrived, the street was blocked off for a just ending farmers market style event. I consider it a stroke of luck. Yes, it would have been even greater luck if I had arrived while the market was still in operation, but had I arrived when the street was clear, I would most likely have at least driven through the district once before stopping for a closer look. Instead, I was directed into a riverside parking lot. I could have driven straight through the lot and gone on my way, but I did have enough sense to not do that.

I actually had no intention of driving through the town without stopping. Back at the JHA conference in Saint Joseph, Missouri, Natchitoches had been mentioned as a possible location for the next conference. It was hardly certain, but the name was in my head and I was certainly going to take a look. Getting shunted into the parking area caused my first look at the area to be on foot and that was a good thing.

Riverside stage, Natchitoches, LA (May 5, 2018)

Although I didn't know it at the time, much of what I was seeing was just a few months old. Dedication of the Rue Beauport Riverfront project, which included the stage, handicapped access, and more, had taken place on November 16, 2017. I strolled along the river for a bit then climbed to Front Street where the Jefferson Highway once ran.

Front Street, Natchitoches, LA (May 5, 2018)

Front Street is a one sided affair. The west side of the street is lined with restaurants and shops. The east side is open to the river making the recently renovated riverfront essentially the front yard for the historic district of Louisiana's oldest city. One of the businesses on the street is the Kaffie-Frederick General Mercantile Store, the oldest general store in the state.

The uncertainty about whether or not the 2019 Jefferson Highway Association conference will be held here has since been removed. The conference is scheduled for the last week of April.

Following the Jefferson Highway from Winnipeg to New Orleans involves driving south to north through Natchitoches with that riverfront park on the right hand side. In fact, the route maintains that bearing for a few miles north of the city and across the Red River before returning to its southeast course. In the process, it rejoins US 71, which it left way back in Missouri, near the town of Clarence.

Between here and the Atchafalaya River, US-71 basically fills the role that once belonged to the Jefferson Highway. I would leave the US route to drive older roads through places like Montgomery and Colfax but US 71 was never far away.

Old Jefferson Highway, Montgomery, LA (May 5, 2018)

US 71 south of Clarence is two lanes and a very pleasant drive, but it gets better just north of Montgomery. There a narrow paved road, signed Old Jefferson Highway, veers off to the west and heads on toward the town. There is a bit of a disconnect in Montgomery, but the road and the name continue on the south side of town. All told, this section includes about three miles of drivable Old Jefferson Highway.

Less than a mile beyond the return to US 71, a giant folk art installation appeared at roadside. The picture shows just a fraction of the display, but you get the idea.

Folk art near Montgomery, LA (May 5, 2018)

US 71 near Morrow, LA (May 5, 2018)

One of my departures from US 71 was to drive through Alexandria. After rejoining the US route south of town, I pretty much stuck with it to Lebeau. The Jefferson Highway and the original US 71 curved to the east at Lebeau, but the current US 71 goes straight ahead to its end point at Krotz Springs.

LA 10 near Palmetto, LA (May 5, 2018)

The road east of Lebeau is now LA 10. It has a gap at the Atchafalaya River. Prior to 2010, the gap was closed by a ferry at Melville. The Jefferson Highway and the early US 71 also crossed the river by ferry. US 71 was moved to its current alignment in 1936 following the building of a bridge at Krotz Springs.

I was not trying to drive every inch of original Jefferson Highway alignment. For one thing, I haven't the slightest idea where some of those inches even are. But I did want to drive as much of the route as I reasonably could. I figured I could drive LA 10 to the river's west bank, then drive south to the bridge and back up the other side; Ten miles each way. Both Garmin and Google indicated this was possible.

Some may think that a twenty mile drive to get to a river with no bridge and no ferry is pretty dumb. Maybe so, but I assure you I have done many things much dumber. In fact, I did something that I consider really dumb when I reached Melville. Actually, the really dumb part was what I didn't do. I did not get a picture of or even a look at the river or the former ferry site. When I reached the road I intended to follow south, I simply turned onto it and kept driving. That's no doubt what was plotted in the GPS, but I should have had the sense to drive a couple hundred yards beyond the turn to see what was there. I didn't.

The drive south went smoothly. I reached US 190, crossed the river, and started looking for a place to turn left. I found none. What's more, I was on a highway with a center divider and no place to pull off – for six miles. When I did eventually pull over and analyzed my situation, I discovered I had covered more than half the distance between Krotz Springs and Livonia where I had planned to reconnect with the "normal" route after the ferry-less diversion. I could either turn around, drive back to the Atchafalaya, hope to find the road north, and reach Livonia after roughly thirty-five miles, or I could reach it by driving forward five miles.

After establishing my ability to do dumb things, I expect some will be surprised, and maybe even disappointed, by my decision to take the shorter path. That was definitely the sensible choice but it magnified my earlier dumb move at Melville. I now continued toward NOLA without visiting either side of the former ferry site and having bypassed nearly twenty miles of known Jefferson Highway.

I spent the night in Port Allen and crossed the Mississippi into Baton Rouge in the morning. This is the river that I walked across on a log fifteen days earlier. I could have done it without the log except for my aversion to frozen toes. That log was maybe thirty feet long. The bridge I used to reach Baton Rouge measures more than a mile in length. Temperature wasn't much of a deterrent to wading. I don't know what the water temperature was but the air above it was around 80° F. There were other considerations, however. The river itself is about a half-mile wide here and more than 30 feet deep.

Huey P. Long Bridge, Baton Rouge, LA (May 6, 2018)

Note that there are two Huey P. Long bridges in Louisiana. This one, built in 1940, and the over four mile long one in New Orleans built in 1935.

Jefferson Highway sign, Baton Rouge, LA (May 6, 2018)

Inside Baton Rouge, the original Jefferson Highway name is used for part of the route. It shows up on several signs at street intersections and even appears on at least one big overhead sign.

The Jefferson Highway and LA 73 follow an eastward arc between Baton Rouge and Geismar. Those two cities on the Mississippi are LA 73's endpoints. The Jefferson Highway name is essentially maintained all the way although it does sometimes get the word 'Old' placed in front of it. After it returns to the Mississippi River at Geismar, the Jefferson Highway pretty much hugs the river all the way to about a mile beyond the other Huey P. Long bridge.

The river and the road have moved around somewhat over the last century so I can't claim that the path I followed matched the original Jefferson Highway path. All I can say is that I stayed as close to the river as possible. The road probably follows a slightly different path than it did a century ago, and it definitely doesn't look the same. For one thing, huge levies have been constructed to keep the river from encroaching on the road. While this blocks a view of the river, both the grass covered levies and the asphalt pavement are well maintained so that the drive, if not exactly scenic, is far from ugly.

The Mississippi River is big and the bridges that cross it are long and tall to accommodate the commercial vessels traveling on it. Hugging the river means passing underneath those bridges. The first one I drove under was the Sunshine Bridge carrying LA 70. The Huey P. Long Bridge at New Orleans would be the fourth. In between were the Veterans Memorial Bridge, which carries LA-3213, and the Luling Bridge, carrying I-310.

LA 70 Sunshine Bridge near Union, LA (Jul 6, 2018)

It isn't constantly in your face, but this is basically a big shipping corridor. Grain and oil storage tanks are sprinkled throughout along with some oil refineries. The industrial appearance is tempered a lot by the green of the levies and the fact that most of those tanks and associated gear are well maintained and kept looking as good as possible. Even so, it isn't the sort of place I would normally associate with tourism. I was not expecting any sort of roadside attraction at all which made finding one entirely too big and too colorful to miss a real surprise. I didn't see it in time to stop, but the bright blue sure caught my eye and I turned around at the first opportunity.

I pulled into the parking lot and read signs to learn that I was at the San Francisco Plantation and that tours of the manor house were available. This was a genuine Jefferson Highway tourist attraction. I wanted to take a tour, but I was at a point where I really did have something of a schedule to keep, and had used up much of the slack. I reluctantly pulled back onto the road without a tour which means what I do know about the plantation was learned later from the internet.

San Francisco Plantation, Garyville, LA (May 6, 2018)

The building was completed in 1855 with skilled slaves doing most of the work. Of course, slaves did most of the work on the entire sugar plantation. Edmond Marmillion, who had the house built, died within a year of its completion and other family members had their share of misfortune, too. In the mid-1970s, the house was restored to its appearance just prior to the Civil War including the bright exterior colors, interior frescoes, and other decorations. The more I've learned, the more disappointed I've become about missing that tour.

San Francisco Plantation is between the Veterans Memorial Bridge and the Luling Bridge. I found another roadside attraction between the Luling Bridge and the Huey P. Long Bridge. Now called Kenner, it's a spot that has attracted travelers for quite some time. French explorer René-Robert Cavelier, Sieur de La Salle landed here in 1682 and claimed pretty much the entire Mississippi River basin for France. He named it Louisiana after his king.

Prize fight monument, Kenner, LA (May 6, 2018)

Then a couple of Englishmen came to town in 1870. That was just fifteen years after Kennerville was founded. In what is referred to as the "first world championship heavyweight prize fight held in the United States", Jem Mace defeated Tom Allen to claim the championship and the $2,500 prize. The event drew about a thousand spectators from New Orleans.

Mississippi River, Kenner, LA (May 6, 2018)

I'd been catching glimpses of the river as I drove along but had not had a good look in a long time. In Kenner I got a very good look and even took a picture. To put something of a scale on things, I looked up the pictured freighter (Mardinik) to learn it is 181 meters (595 feet) long , 30 meters (98 feet) wide, and tall enough to make anybody on one of those bridges nervous. Trees along the bank were partially submerged so I assume the river was a little higher than normal.

Canal Street, New Orleans, LA (May 6, 2018)

The end was near. From Kenner, it was just a few miles to the left turn that started me toward downtown New Orleans. A few more miles on various city streets brought me to the northeast end of Canal Street. Cruising nearly the full length of this wide boulevard seemed a fitting way to prepare myself for the trip's finale. The Canal Street photo was taken at Villere Street. Nine blocks later I made the closing Jefferson Highway turn onto Saint Charles Street.

JH terminus marker, New Orleans, LA (May 6, 2018)

Terminus marker with palm trees, New Orleans, LA (May 6, 2018)

I spotted the Jefferson Highway terminus marker at the next corner and documented the pass with a couple of shaky snapshots. Then I parked nearby and walked back for some better pictures. The marker and the palm trees standing across the street meant my Pine to Palm journey was complete.

It had begun seventeen days earlier inside the Canadian province of Manitoba, and had included seven US states not counting that tiny corner of North Dakota. There was a two day pause in Missouri for the Jefferson Highway Association Conference leaving fifteen travel days to account for the 2276 miles of the calculated route.

With twenty degrees of latitude separating the highway's ends, a goodly range of weather is to be expected, and I certainly saw variety. I suppose I could have done without all that rain in Texas but it really did no harm and didn't even alter my activities significantly. I did not encounter any falling snow during the "official" drive from Winnipeg, but did on the way there, and I saw sizable mounds of the stuff well into Iowa as I moved south. Runoff from those mounds made some of the unpaved roads and paths a little more challenging than they probably would have been otherwise. Unpaved miles, as I mentioned earlier, made up 72 of the 2276 total. The vast majority of the drive was dry with a real mix of clear sky and clouds and temperatures that ranged all over the thermometer.

Signage varied at least as much as the weather. Iowa, Missouri, and Oklahoma do a decent job of marking much of the old route with signs or striped poles. The Jefferson name appears on quite a few streets and roads along the way though that's hardly a reliable way of identifying old JH pathways. In short, it's simply not possible to follow the historic route for any distance without a little help and pre-trip planning.

I had quite a bit of help and did a fair amount of planning, and still missed bits here and there. Some I knew about when I did it, others I discovered by chatting with folks in Saint Joseph or elsewhere, and some I learned of only after I got home. Plus, there are no doubt plenty of missed spots I just haven't realized yet. That's how road trips work. A road fan's standard response to learning that something was missed is, "That's just a reason to go back."

Road fans also know that any worthwhile road trip has a little serendipity involved. On this one the Saint Pie cross in Manitoba and Val's Rapid Serv in Minnesota immediately come to mind. Of course, now that you know about them you won't be surprised by them, and you'll just have to find your own serendipity. On the Jefferson Highway, I don't think it will be much of a problem.

Resources

Jefferson Highway Association – The association's website (https://www.JeffersonHighway.org) contains lots of information about the association and the highway. In particular, the "Maps" page offers information about the route including links to the Mike Curtis map and Jane Ballard Oklahoma tour guide. The association also maintains a Facebook page (https://www.facebook.com/Jefferson-Highway-129069972974/) where comments may be made and questions asked.

Lincoln Highway Association – The map for the 2017 Northwoods Auto Tour, which included the Jefferson Highway between Colo, IA, and Winnipeg, MB, is available at https://www.lincolnhighwayassoc.org/tour/2017/map/

The Jefferson Highway: Blazing the Way from Winnipeg to New Orleans – This book by Lyell D. Henry Jr. contains an excellent history of the original 1915 Jefferson Highway Association along with details of the highway's route through Iowa.

Jefferson Highway All the Way – The route plotted, and mostly followed, for the trip described in this book is online at https://tinyurl.com/y233tmrb

ABOUT THE AUTHOR

Denny Gibson is a retired software engineer living on the outskirts of Cincinnati, Ohio. He is addicted to driving two-lane highways and, since 1999, has documented his travels on them at DennyGibson.com. His photographs and writings have appeared in other travel books and magazines. He is the author of *By Mopar to the Golden Gate* which tells the story of driving the Lincoln Highway during its centennial year in a fifty year old car.

Made in the USA
Monee, IL
18 December 2024

74287852R00085